Supporting Children
Young People in Schc

This book explores the diverse ways in which practitioners can support students' learning, enabling them to develop and flourish in the school setting. Chapters bring together various theoretical approaches, draw on case studies from practice and foreground the concrete ways in which practitioners might respond to the specific needs of children.

Maintaining a strong link with current policy and curricula, each chapter takes a detailed and nuanced approach to a different aspect of pupil support, whilst reflective questions, activities and suggestions for further reading encourage the reader to reflect, re-consider and delve deeper into key topics. Areas addressed include:

- theories of child and adolescent development
- managing student behaviour and building positive relationships
- working with pupils with special educational needs
- making use of assessment and evaluation
- furthering professional skills and career progression.

An accessible yet comprehensive guide to a wide range of key issues, this book will provide Foundation Degree students, teaching assistants and practitioners working in a range of educational settings with essential support as they progress from study into practice.

Allison Tatton is currently Head of Early Childhood Education and Care at Newman University, UK. She has led the Foundation Degree for Teaching and Learning Support at the University for 12 years.

Clare Bright is Senior Lecturer in Education and Multi-professional Practice at Newman University, UK. She has over 20 years of experience of primary teaching.

Lorraine Thomas is currently Dean of the Faculty of Education at Newman University, UK. She gained 14 years of experience teaching in secondary schools before entering higher education.

Supporting Children and Young People in Schools

A Guide for Foundation Degree Students

Edited by Allison Tatton, Clare Bright
and Lorraine Thomas

Routledge
Taylor & Francis Group

LONDON AND NEW YORK

First published 2018
by Routledge
2 Park Square, Milton Park, Abingdon, Oxon OX14 4RN

and by Routledge
711 Third Avenue, New York, NY 10017

Routledge is an imprint of the Taylor & Francis Group, an informa business

British Library Cataloguing in Publication Data
A catalogue record for this book is available from the British Library

Library of Congress Cataloging in Publication Data
A catalog record has been requested for this book

ISBN: 9781138244603 (hbk)
ISBN: 9781138244610 (pbk)
ISBN: 9781315276854 (ebk)

Typeset in Melior
by Swales & Willis Ltd, Exeter, Devon, UK
Printed by CPI Group (UK) Ltd, Croydon CR0 4YY

Contents

Figures and tables

Figures

Tables

Foreword

At the time of writing this foreword, it is increasingly obvious to me that the study and development of thinking, doing and improving professionalism in the field of pupil support in the school setting are both timely as well as an important but overdue development. Recurring political attitudes to this area of provision, after the transforming school workforce reforms at the turn of the century in England and Wales, have since attracted less funding, fewer resources and in the opinion of many, an inappropriate level of invested status, attention, priority and regard. This is deeply ironic given the mounting crisis in teacher recruitment and retention in the English school system today.

There is a clear and present need for more work in a range of professional knowledge across the whole spectrum of school and teaching support. The chapters in this book reflect this wide range of topics in a balanced and meaningful way. This breadth of subject matter includes consideration of educational policy, the role of the teaching assistant (TA), the place and value of reflective practice, and the theory of child and adolescent development. It looks at supporting professional core skills, understanding and delivery of the contemporary curriculum. Further consideration is given to important pedagogic aspects of the curriculum involving technology, behaviour and relationships, as well as a need to know about professional leadership, special educational needs and disabilities (SEND), inclusion and diversity, assessment and evaluation. As an individual's study moves toward undertaking a research project, there is help with the next steps in developing professional practice when working with families, children and young people. Relevance, pragmatism and accessibility are key themes both for working practice and study.

This book is therefore a welcome contribution to the literature and while the authors' intentions are to collectively provide an entry-level text aimed at new students taking up study at university, and who are likely to have been out of education for a while (usually mature students), it will provide essential, accessible and relevant reading for working practitioners returning to a CPD project. It is likely that those teaching the new T Level examination in schools/colleges in the new post-16 curriculum in England will find this book an invaluable resource. The first T Level, a vocational learning route for education and childcare, is to include T Levels for para-professional work/roles such as nursery assistant, early years officer, teaching assistant and youth worker.

Lastly the final chapter, dealing with reflective practice, aptly and usefully points up and reinforces the central place of reflection in continuing professional learning/development. Reflection is a vital part in learning from experience and the past, before taking decisions and moving forward. Career success, practitioner knowledge and expertise, as well as professional credentials, are all shaped or determined in this way. This book offers a very useful contribution to establishing the platform upon which to further develop this professional expertise and understanding. The process of learning in this way is, or at least should be, an enthralling but never-ending story.

Professor Steve Rayner PhD

Acknowledgements

We would like to thank all of the contributors to this book, especially our student contributors who have written many of the case studies based on their everyday experiences in schools. We would also like to thank all of those students with whom we have worked over the years, for their inspiration, insight and commitment to their studies. We applaud your resilience and ability to juggle work, family and relationships as well as study.

Abbreviations

ADHD	Attention deficit hyperactivity disorder
ASD	Autistic spectrum disorder
CA	Classroom assistant
CPD	Continuing professional development
DCSF	Department for Children, Schools and Families (*now* Department for Education)
EAL	English as an additional language
ECM	Every child matters
EYFS	Early years foundation stage
FSM	Free school meals
GCSE	General certificate of secondary education
HLTA	Higher level teaching assistant
ICT	Information and communication technology
IEP	Individual education plan
IT	Information technology
LAD	Language acquisition device
LASS	Language acquisition support system
LEA	Local Education Authority
LSA	Learning support assistant
MAT	Multi-academy trust
NASC	National award for special educational needs co-ordination
Ofsted	Office for Standards in Education, Children's Services and Skills
QCA	Qualifications and curriculum authority
QTS	Qualified teacher status
PDA	Pathological demand avoidance
PISA	Programme for international student assessment
PPA	Planning, preparation and assessment
PSHE	Personal, social and health education

SATs	Standard attainment tests
SENco	Special educational needs co-ordinator
TA	Teaching assistant
VAK	Visual, auditory and kinaesthetic
VLE	Virtual learning environment
ZAD	Zone of actual development
ZPD	Zone of proximal development

Contributors

Parminder Assi

Parminder originally worked as a primary and secondary teacher predominantly in the West Midlands area. An interest in language teaching led to work in an advisory role in Birmingham LEA and then to managing a team of peripatetic language support teachers in Sandwell LEA, before becoming a member of the Ofsted inspector team. In her higher education role, Parminder has taught on a range of modules on the BA Combined Honours Education Studies and Single Honours Studies in Primary Education, postgraduate programmes and Initial Teacher Training programmes. Parminder has extensive experience in advisory work in the areas of equality issues and diversity, with specific attention to learners for whom English is an additional language (EAL) and in widening participation in higher education. Parminder's research interests include the areas of pupil attainment and assessment, participation and educational equity, and she is currently exploring the area of baseline assessment in reception classrooms within primary schools.

John Bayley

John spent 29 years in primary schools, his last six as headteacher of a school in a very deprived part of the West Midlands. Since 2002 he has been Senior Lecturer in Education Studies and is currently course leader for Newman University's degree in Studies in Primary Education. His main interests are in the areas of creativity, access and inclusion.

Jane Beniston

Jane has worked in primary education for over 10 years, first as a reception class teacher, then moving on to foundation stage co-ordinator, running a new 60-place nursery and finally as acting headteacher in a variety of different schools. Her roles within these schools included RE co-ordinator and maths leader within Key Stages 1 and 2. Jane has worked at Newman University for 14 years, teaching across undergraduate, foundation degree and masters provision within the School of Education. Her main teaching lies within the Early Childhood Education and Care programme. Jane also led the Early Years Initial Teacher Training programme (EYITT) leading to Early Years Teacher status (EYT). This involves liaison with local settings to provide placements for trainees to teach across the babies, toddlers and young children range (ages 0–5).

Clare Bright

Clare is a senior lecturer in Education and Multi-professional Practice at Newman University. Before working in higher education, she was a Special Educational Needs Co-ordinator in a primary school and she has over 20 years of experience in primary teaching. She has a particular interest in SEND and inclusion and teaches across a range of programmes including the MA Education, Studies in Primary Education and the Foundation Degree for Teaching and Learning Support.

Stephen Dixon

Dr Stephen Dixon is a senior lecturer in Education and Multi Professional Practice at Newman University and teaches on a range of courses, including the BA (Hons) in Education Studies, MA (Education) and the professional doctorate. Previously a senior lecturer in ICT, Stephen specialises in E-learning and the use of multimedia in learning and teaching, with a particular focus on web-based and audio-visual materials. He also runs modules on the social, political and ethical considerations of using technology. He has acted as external consultant for other universities, and is a Fellow of the Higher Education Academy.

Cheryl Hedges

Cheryl is a senior lecturer in Education and Multi-professional Practice at Newman University. She is an experienced secondary practitioner focussing on post-16 provision. She taught and examined in sociology, psychology and politics at Level 3 within school and further education settings. She has senior leadership experience as director of post-16 education, with a passion for collaboration and widening participation. Cheryl was a coach and mentor across leadership programmes within school and pastoral leader for post-16 students in large and varied secondary schools. In addition, before taking up her post in higher education she worked as an educational advisor on curriculum creation and formation for secondary headteachers. Her research interests include gender, class and critical pedagogy and adult education. She is a Fellow of the HEA.

Angela Sawyer

Angela Sawyer is currently working as a senior lecturer in Primary English on the PGCE and undergraduate programmes for Initial Teacher Education and has contributed to the Foundation Degree in Teaching and Learning at Newman University, Birmingham. After studying at Wolverhampton University, she spent over 20 years teaching in a large, inner-city primary school in Birmingham, taking on extra management roles alongside a diverse range of curricular responsibilities. After participating in a research project relating to the use of Bollywood films to promote children's literacy, she developed an interest in the use of visual literacy to support language learning amongst children with English as an Additional Language. In 2012, she was appointed as a senior lecturer at Newman University and has recently completed her Master's dissertation in the role of performance poetry in the primary classroom. Her areas of interest include research into the use of technology to support literacy and, after a recent visit to Sweden, the use of the outdoors to develop and enhance literacy opportunities.

Andrew Sheehan

Andrew originally worked as a biomedical scientist for nine years before entering the teaching profession. His work in histopathology focussed on the diagnosis and prognosis of tumours using electron microscopy and immunohistochemistry. Over the years, Andrew has taught in secondary schools, a moderate learning difficulty school and primary schools across inner-city Walsall and Birmingham, before entering higher education. He is passionate about science and quality science teaching that introduces pupils to working scientifically from a young age. Andrew currently lectures on undergraduate BA (QTS) Primary Education and PGCE Primary (QTS) programmes, the Foundation Degree for Teaching and Learning Support and the Subject Knowledge Enhancement course for Chemistry. His research interests include neuromuscular diseases and their impact on student learning and educational experience.

Allison Tatton

After working in banking for 13 years Allison changed careers and trained to become a primary school teacher specialising in early childhood. She worked in the Foundation Stage and Key Stage 1 in several schools across Birmingham and the West Midlands region before taking up a post at Newman University in 2005 funded by the European Social Fund to research skills gaps and training needs of the early childhood workforce. She has worked in higher education for 13 years and led the Foundation Degree for Teaching and Learning Support at Newman University for 12 years. Her research interests include fostering families, children's physical activity levels in the foundation stage, the early childhood workforce and children's literacy development. She is currently Head of Early Childhood Education and Care at Newman University.

Jacky Taylor

Jacky developed a fascination around the process of learning and how it is acquired after the birth of her twin sons in 1990. Jacky has worked with families and children for Birmingham City Council, culminating in managing a team of practitioners working in schools, children's centres, refuges and health settings where her role was to support families and young children's development and learning, in particular targeting the inclusion of harder-to-reach families such as prisoner families and traveller families. Jacky's research interests include exploring the experiences and perceptions of contemporary fathers through the role of professional practice and the concept of aspiration in contemporary parents and professionals. Jacky currently works at Newman University specialising in safeguarding, educational leadership and multi-agency working. Her current research is in the area of liminality in higher education students through the lens of aspiration. She also mentors learners with their Teaching and Learning Academy (TLA) qualifications as well as co-ordinating the Early Years Foundation Degree programme.

Lorraine Thomas

Lorraine's first post was as a teacher of English as a Foreign Language in Cartagena, Spain. After completing a PGCE in Modern Foreign Languages (MFL), she then worked in secondary schools in the West Midlands for 14 years, where she achieved several regional and national awards for innovative practice, including the European Award for Languages. Lorraine has held a range of posts in higher education: Director of Postgraduate and Professional Development Studies in the School of Education at the University of Wolverhampton; Head of Centre: Secondary and Post-compulsory initial teacher education (ITE) in the Institute of Education at the University of Worcester; Principal Lecturer in Higher Education in the Academic Development and Practice Unit at the University of Worcester; CPD Programme Leader and then Associate Dean in the School of Education at Newman University. Since moving to higher education, Lorraine has led a range of undergraduate and postgraduate programmes, in addition to securing many successful bids and consultancy activities. Lorraine is currently Dean of the Faculty of Education at Newman University.

Ian Tinley

Ian has taught in primary schools within the West Midlands and Universities of Wolverhampton and Warwick, where he led postgraduate and undergraduate primary mathematics. Ian has also worked with Primary National Strategies undertaking research and development. He led West Midlands Primary Teach First whilst at the University of Warwick from 2012 to 2013 before moving to Newman in 2013 to join the primary mathematics team. His research interests lie in the transition from mental to written calculations although lately he is exploring the retention rates of males within primary ITE.

Chris Watts

Chris originally trained as a primary teacher and has worked with children, parents and teachers in schools across the West Midlands for many years. He has also worked as a teacher in Further Education and currently teaches on ITE courses. Chris has been at Newman University for 12 years. He has a particular interest in working with refugee children.

Introduction

Allison Tatton, Clare Bright and Lorraine Thomas

If you are reading this book (or intend to read this book) there is every chance that you are studying – or are about to study for – a Foundation Degree. However, this book will also be useful to you if you are undertaking any course of study relating to working with children or young people in an educational setting. There are sections which ask you to focus specifically on your role in school but there are also sections which will provide you with useful information on a whole range of education-related topics.

The book is aimed at people who support children's learning in schools and other educational settings. These colleagues are more recently referred to as 'Teaching Assistants', or TAs for short, which is the term we have chosen to use throughout the book, although we recognise that a whole range of titles is used to describe support staff in schools and other settings. These include Learning Support Assistants, Learning Mentors, Classroom Assistants, Inclusion Assistants, Inclusion Workers, EAL Teaching Assistants, Nursery Nurses etc. We apologise if the exact title for your role has not been included here but there are too many to mention them all. Each of these titles may have the emphasis on a slightly different aspect of the role but essentially the role involves supporting children and/or young people's learning.

Sections and contents

To help you navigate through the book we have divided it into four sections. The first section relates to 'professional issues'. Within this section, Chapter 1 considers the role of TAs in schools but also the role of support staff in other areas. Here we consider the historical development of the TA role and reflect on some of the attributes TAs need in order to undertake their complex role in schools effectively. In Chapter 2 we reflect on educational policy and explore some of the changes and background to the educational context for children and young people. This chapter primarily relates to the education system in England but some of the information and underpinning principles are applicable to other parts of the United Kingdom. The final chapter in this section highlights the importance of reflective practice for TAs and anyone working in educational settings. It explores a range of factors that impact on learning and identifies the study skills that will support you if you are undertaking a Foundation Degree.

The second section, which is the largest, considers 'curriculum issues'. This section starts in Chapter 4 by looking at some basic areas of child development and some of the key theorists relevant to each of the topics covered. These topics include language development, social development and moral development as well as areas such as personal, social and emotional development. We could not hope, in one short chapter, to provide you with all you need to know, especially on this topic. There are numerous excellent texts on all areas of child development and we strongly suggest that you consider reading some of these. Chapter 5 provides a brief overview of curriculum development in England in both primary and secondary schools and makes comparisons with Scotland and Wales. It explores how children's learning is supported through creativity. This section then moves on to consider how TAs support the core skills of English, maths and science in the classroom. The authors have provided some useful examples of activities you might carry out as part of your practice. We recognise that technology is also considered a key aspect of teaching and learning and we devote Chapter 7 to 'Children and technology'. This chapter considers how as a TA you are expected to support ICT both as a discrete subject, and also embedded within other curriculum areas, and where it is used to support learning. The final chapter within this section considers the 'hot topics' of assessment and evaluation. We look at formative and summative assessment and the purpose of these. The chapter also covers why assessment is important and the purpose of marking and giving feedback on children's and young people's work.

The third section considers something that most of you will be very familiar with: supporting pupils' learning needs. Chapter 9 considers the 'tricky' topic of working with parents and in particular those parents who are considered harder to reach. It also considers how we might engage those parents who appear unwilling to work with us on a regular basis. It explores some of the reasons why this might be, as well as offering some strategies for how we might work more effectively with parents. In Chapter 10 we explore different definitions of inclusion and introduce the legislative frameworks for special educational needs and disabilities (SEND). A range of learner needs are recognised and strategies to support them are discussed. We also consider some of the barriers to effective support. Chapter 11 looks at the role of TAs in working with pupils who present challenging behaviours. We look at children whose behaviour is 'difficult' and suggest some reasons for this. This chapter identifies strategies for managing behaviour and includes some reflection on the importance of effective relationships. Chapter 12 considers the languages spoken and used in schools by children described as having English as an additional language (EAL). It explores how children acquire multiple languages and provides a simple review of language acquisition theories. How language shapes learner identity is also discussed.

The fourth and final section asks you to consider your own professional development. Many foundation degrees require students to undertake a small-scale research project as one of its final assessments. This is often the culmination of your degree and gives you the opportunity to study an area of your choosing in significant depth. Chapter 13 gives some useful advice on negotiating and completing what may be one of the most challenging aspects of your study at the higher education level to date. The final chapter encourages you to consider what you are going to do once you have completed your Foundation Degree. We hope that you have 'caught the learning bug' and will go on to complete a full Honours Degree and Higher Degree. You may also wish to gain Qualified Teacher Status. This chapter offers some current and helpful advice as to how you might achieve this. However, you must remember that going on to gain QTS is a fast-changing landscape and while this information is accurate at the time of going to press, there may be other routes open to you, or indeed some routes may no longer be available, when you read this. Therefore it is important to ensure you research this area well and in good time to get in your applications to your chosen institution or UCAS.

How to use this text

This is not the kind of text that you start at page 1 and read through to the end. We expect students/readers to 'dip into and out of' this text. Therefore, while we make links between the chapters so that you can easily locate more information on particular subjects, each chapter is self-contained and can be read on its own.

We have also deliberately made each chapter quite short as we know how busy TAs are. We want you to have access to some of the key ideas and thoughts relating to each of the topics covered. One text could not hope to be able to cover everything you need in order to study for your Foundation Degree and therefore each of the authors has provided a list of further reading where you will be able to delve deeper into the key topics within this text. We strongly recommend that you seek out and use some of these books and websites as they will provide wider reading which will be invaluable to your study. The authors of each of the chapters have also used case studies within the chapters. Many of the case studies used relate to real-life situations and have been written by students who have undertaken or are currently studying for a Foundation Degree. The case studies will help you relate what you are reading to your own role, although we are sure you will be able to make links between much of what is said in the chapters and your daily practice.

The authors have also identified reflection points for you to stop and think about while you are reading. We would encourage you not to skip over these activities but to spend time engaging with them. Some of the reflection points will support you in developing your own ideas, which is a key part of becoming a student in higher education. Others will encourage you to reflect on your practice and to consider why and how you do what you do. Other reflection points have been designed to support you in relating theory to practice, which is a key skill on many courses. All of the authors and editors of this book have worked with Foundation Degree students for many years and therefore have a good understanding of the complexities of combining study, work, family, friends, relationships and other aspects of busy lives successfully.

This text would not have been possible without the support of many colleagues. We would also like to thank the contributors for the time, expertise and hard work they have invested in the production of this book. We have covered a wide range of topics but if you have any ideas or suggestions about what you would find useful please do contact us and let us know. We would love to hear from you. We hope you will find this text useful and we wish you every success in your studies.

PART I
Professional issues

1 The role of the Teaching Assistant

Allison Tatton and Clare Bright

CHAPTER OVERVIEW AND AIMS

- To explore some of the issues and policy changes that have contributed to the development of the role of Teaching Assistants (TAs)

- To encourage reflection on practice and consider how the TA role has changed in the recent past

- To consider the personal skills and qualities required to undertake such a diverse range of responsibilities

- To explore some of the challenges faced by TAs

Introduction

This chapter will introduce you to how the role of support staff in schools, in particular TAs, has developed in recent years and will also consider some of the reasons why these changes have taken place. We shall explore the diverse roles that TAs undertake and some of the challenges they face in carrying out these roles. We also reflect on the skills and qualities required to carry out the role effectively.

Context

As we discussed in the introduction to this book, the term 'TA' includes practitioners working in a wide range of roles. Traditionally, support staff were more likely to be employed to support younger children and were known as nursery nurses.

Later, as a result of some of the reforms detailed below, their titles changed and they have since been referred to as Teaching Assistants (TAs), Classroom Assistants (CAs), Learning Support Assistants (LSAs), Specialist Teaching Assistants (STAs) and Higher Level Teaching Assistants (HLTAs) alongside other terms (Cajkler *et al.*, 2007). The number of support staff in schools has increased significantly in recent years from 81,900 staff who were classed as 'non-teaching', but who worked directly with children in 1997 (DfEE, 1997) to 235,000 full-time-equivalent school support staff in 2016 (DfE, 2016). This increase can largely be attributed to changes in government policy in three key areas: firstly, as a result of education reform in the 1980s; secondly, the desire to improve standards, particularly in literacy and numeracy in primary schools; and finally, workload agreements for teachers in the 1990s. These are considered in more detail below.

In 1997 an inclusive education agenda was introduced which aimed to educate as many children as possible, including those with special educational needs (SEN), in mainstream schools (DfEE, 1997). TAs were employed to support the inclusion of children with SEN in mainstream classrooms and this caused the number of TAs to increase dramatically (Walton and Goddard, 2013). This was seen as the 'root cause' of the growth in TAs and also resulted in the first changes to their role. In 2010 there were 48,100 TAs who were employed specifically to support children who had SEN (DCSF, 2010). We look at this aspect of the TA role again in Chapter 10.

The second reason, which relates predominantly to primary schools, was the desire to raise standards in literacy and numeracy. In order to achieve this, the government introduced the National Strategies for Literacy and Numeracy (DfEE, 1998; 1999). These strategies required a complex system of classroom management and more than one adult to teach each class. TAs were recruited to work with small groups of children in classrooms and often worked with lower-ability groups. The standards agenda and accountability will be discussed again in Chapter 2.

The third factor was due to workload agreements for teachers. During the 1990s the workload of teachers had increased to such an extent that PricewaterhouseCoopers LLP was commissioned by the government to undertake an investigation into teacher workloads, which led to the National Agreement (DfES, 2003) to remodel the school workforce. One of the recommendations was to deploy school support staff more effectively and it was proposed that they should take over some of the administrative tasks traditionally carried out by teachers (Sharples *et al.*, 2015). TAs began to take on greater teaching roles, allowing teachers guaranteed non-contact time for planning, preparation and assessment (PPA) and in order to reduce workloads for teachers.

The above reforms gave rise to the change in the role of many TAs who, in a relatively short period of time, have gone from classroom helpers to important members of an educational team (Chambers, 2015). In the 1980s TAs were often not allowed to undertake a teaching role in classrooms but carried out art and craft activities with children and typically maintained display boards and ran the school library. At the time of writing, however, it is quite common within primary schools to have a full-time TA in every class, with additional TAs employed to cover specific roles. In secondary schools, TAs can often have specific expertise in curriculum areas and are assigned to subject areas or departments (Blatchford *et al.*, 2012). Today TAs can also often be found in all age phases, leading curriculum areas and developments; heading school-based initiatives; working with professionals from other services; and teaching whole class sessions, in addition to many of the roles that they have traditionally undertaken.

REFLECTION POINTS

- How has your role changed since you first started working in schools?

- How do you feel about the responsibility you have for children's learning?

- What part of your job do you enjoy the most?

- How do you think you would feel working in the type of role detailed above, where you were not generally involved in learning and teaching but did mainly administrative and sometimes creative tasks such as photocopying, displays or art activities?

ACTIVITY

- Talk to one of your colleagues who has been a teaching assistant longer than you. Try to find someone who has been in the role for a number of years. Ask them how their role has changed.

Towards a typology

In the early 2000s the Department for Education and Skills (DfES) set up a working group to consider TA roles and broadly categorised the role of support staff in schools into three groups: roles supporting pupils, such as children with SEN or who were bilingual; more technical roles supporting the curriculum; and roles supporting the school, such as secretaries and bursars, but the boundaries between these were described as being 'rather porous' – meaning that some roles involved aspects of others (Kerry, 2005). Kerry attempted to develop a typology of the roles TAs undertake, focussing on levels of responsibility ranging from what was somewhat unkindly termed 'dogsbody' or 'pig ignorant peasant' through to 'mobile paraprofessional' (Kerry, 2005).

The role described by Kerry as 'dogsbody or pig ignorant peasant' is characterised by TAs who typically carry out manual and/or menial tasks such as the washing of paint pots, backing of art work and generally clearing up. In our experience there are now very few TAs currently employed in this type of role. Kerry's typology culminated in what he terms 'mobile paraprofessional' and, he claimed, is typified by status of Higher Level Teaching Assistant (HLTA) (Kerry, 2005). More recent research by Blatchford *et al.* (2012) identified seven 'post titles' but found that within these post titles the staff were engaged in similar activities. The formulation of the National Agreement in 2003 resulted in a lack of clarity of teacher and TA roles, giving rise to concerns over professional status and job 'boundaries' (Blatchford *et al.*, 2012).

As a direct result of the National Agreement (DfES, 2003) and the Every Child Matters (DfES, 2003) agenda, the HLTA role was introduced in 2003. (The philosophy behind the HTLA role will be discussed further in Chapter 2.) The role requires a basic level of education, plus additional training and evidence that candidates have achieved an appropriate level. This training is below the level of Qualified Teacher Status (QTS). Initially, government funding was available to support schools and therefore TAs to undertake this training but this was withdrawn in 2012 following the election of the Conservative/Liberal coalition government. It should also be noted that the award of HLTA status did not necessarily entitle the recipient to an HLTA role within a school, nor did it incorporate any higher-level academic qualification.

Qualifications

Currently more and more TAs are either entering the profession with undergraduate degrees or are gaining degree-level qualifications while working as a TA (much like yourself), and there is an argument that school leaders are not making the most of this 'valuable resource' (Russell *et al.*, 2013). Many TAs are also recognising that they have specialist skills which could support them to gain teaching qualifications in the future. While the role of the TA has developed and TAs have become an integral part of classroom life, there is still no minimum entry-level qualification for teaching assistants (Blatchford *et al.*, 2012). According to Higgins and Gulliford (2014), 59% of the TA workforce enters the profession with qualifications at General Certificate of Secondary Education (GCSE) level 2 or below, including English and maths GCSEs (Russell *et al.*, 2013). There are currently no mandatory qualifications for TAs working in schools in England (Blatchford *et al.*, 2012), although increasingly some local authorities and individual schools will specify the qualifications and experience they expect of applicants. Additionally, many TAs do not hold qualifications, including those that are sector-related or level 2 qualifications including GCSE English and maths (Russell *et al.*, 2013).

Despite the connection between poor pupil outcomes, if pupils are working with poorly trained and managed TAs (which will be discussed more fully later), continuing professional development (CPD) and training for TAs are still 'patchy' (Cajkler *et al.*, 2007). Giangreco *et al.* in Rose (2010: 254) argue that TAs are often inadequately trained and 'reactively assigned'. A recommendation of the Lamb inquiry into SEN (2009) was that the then Training and Development Agency for Schools (TDA) should develop guidance on the effective deployment of teaching assistants. This was not a new recommendation. Moyles and Suschitzky (1997) made a similar recommendation, identifying that a lack of training and an inadequate career structure were barriers to effective use of TAs, stating that the ad hoc way the role of TAs has developed across the United Kingdom (UK) has resulted in a lack of uniformity surrounding the TA role in the classroom.

Cajkler *et al.* (2007) highlighted that where training was available it was reported to develop staff confidence and knowledge as well as their instructional skills, but training was generally in the form of short courses (one day or less) and was accessed at the discretion of the headteacher. Cajkler *et al.* (2007) also identified that the payment of TAs while undertaking training varied, with a number of the courses conducted exclusively in the TA's own time. Yet as early as 2002, in an evaluation of the impact of TAs, Ofsted reported that the quality of lessons where there was a TA present was better than when a TA was not present. Ofsted (2002) went on to say that when TAs had adequate training, their competence and confidence improved.

CASE STUDY 1.1

A day in the life of a secondary school TA – Sam

My main role is a dual position: I am an English Faculty TA and I also work closely with the Special Educational Needs Co-ordinator (SENCO), managing the provision for Autistic Spectrum Disorder (ASD) pupils at a mainstream secondary school. I am also a form tutor, co-ordinating the pastoral provision for 21 young people.

A typical day consists of: a whole staff briefing at 8.15 am and then straight into the classroom for first lesson by 8.30 am. I meet and greet a pupil with a diagnosis of ASD with Pathological Demand Avoidance (PDA) traits. I then support English lessons which could range from year groups 7–11 and support children with a range of Special

(continued)

(continued)

Educational Needs and Disabilities (SEND) including autism, dyslexia and attention deficit hyperactivity disorder (ADHD). Sometimes this support is 1:1, or it could be a small group or even whole class support and can be inside the classroom or outside, depending on the need. But in my role supporting ASD students in school there is no typical day!

I could be attending a meeting as the professional lead for autism; meeting with an educational psychologist; liaising with the Integrated Disability Service Autism Team for advice and guidance around provision for pupils; meeting with parents; creating and distributing staff training packages and pupil profile documents; writing Individual Education Plans (IEPs); meeting 1:1 with pupils; delivering bespoke personal, social and health education (PSHE) sessions; leading SEND meetings; and a million other things! The teacher and I also meet regularly to discuss individual and whole-class support needs. It is non-stop and there are never enough hours in the day. That said, however challenging it may be, the reward is immense. The reason a TA goes into work is certainly not for the pay – it is definitely the prize of seeing a young person achieve and progress because the right support is in place.

REFLECTION POINTS

- Sam has time to meet regularly with her class teacher to ensure she knows the pupils' specific support needs.

- How does Sam's typical day compare with your day-to-day role?

- Do you feel prepared in advance for the tasks you are asked to undertake?

- What challenges does having a number of roles pose for you?

- What personal skills do you draw upon to manage these challenges?

Challenges faced by TAs

Having explored the development of the TA role, it is clear that the different expectations, demanding working days and inconsistent access to training and support create a number of challenges. Over the last 15 years there have been several research projects into TA deployment and effectiveness (Blatchford *et al.*, 2009; MITA, 2013; Sharples *et al.*, 2015) and these have revealed a number of significant findings:

- The typical deployment and use of TAs, under everyday conditions, is not leading to improvements in academic outcomes.

- TAs help ease teacher workload and stress, reduce classroom disruption and allow teachers more time to teach.

- TAs spend the majority of their time in an informal instructional role supporting pupils with the most need.

- There is mixed evidence to support the view that TA support has a positive impact on 'soft' outcomes. Some evidence suggests TA support may increase dependency.

- TAs tend to be more concerned with task completion and less concerned with developing understanding.

- TAs are not adequately prepared for their role in classrooms and have little time to liaise with teachers.

These findings have led to recommendations that schools carry out a full audit of their current situation and identify how best to deploy their TAs to improve the effectiveness of their practice and minimise the challenges they face on a daily basis. To support this process, and in an attempt to define the role of the TA, the Professional Standards for Teaching Assistants were published in June 2016. These standards, endorsed by representatives from a number of organisations interested in promoting the professional work of TAs, are non-mandatory and non-statutory and have been designed to help to 'define the role and purpose of TAs to ensure that schools can maximise the educational value and contribution of adults working with pupils' (MITA, 2017). Interestingly, the standards have not been promoted by the Department for Education (DfE) despite them having been originally commissioned by the government, and you might like to reflect on why this might be. The standards can be found here:

http://maximisingtas.co.uk/assets/content/ta-standards-final-june2016-1.pdf

You will see that the standards are set out in four themes:

1. Personal and professional conduct
2. Knowledge and understanding
3. Teaching and learning
4. Working with others

The guidance states that the qualities and skills required to work with others were considered so important and distinctive to the TA role as to merit their own theme.

Working with others

Reflecting on your role and looking again at the case study, it is likely that you will come into contact with a number of different people: children, colleagues, parents and professionals from outside your setting, just as Sam does in her daily activities. Working effectively with them involves a range of different personal skills including communication, building relationships and working as a team. To help us understand the skills you use on a daily basis we can look at the work of Daniel Goleman who popularised the term 'emotional intelligence'. He suggested that managing emotions in others is the art of relationships and he described empathy as 'the fundamental people skill' (Goleman, 1996). Interpersonal intelligence was recognised as one of seven intelligences by Howard Gardner in his Theory of Multiple Intelligence. He recognised that humans possess a profile of these intelligences and have varying degrees of strength and weakness in each. Interpersonal intelligence is known as the ability to recognise and interpret the feelings of others (Gardner, 1993).

Communication is a fundamental skill and one that you will have had to develop in order to effectively support children's learning. You will also realise that effective communication with your colleagues is an essential aspect of your role. Obviously the language used in communication is important, but so are the messages indicated through the tone of voice and other non-verbal signals. As a practitioner in school you will be aware of the need to recognise, interpret and act on the thoughts, feelings and meanings conveyed, and you will become skilled at responding appropriately to the needs of each individual you work with. Research into the practice of TAs is not always positive in terms of the quality of interactions with pupils. It has been observed that TAs sometimes 'close down' a pupil's responses but there are also positive outcomes from having longer interactions with TAs than are often possible with teachers in busy classrooms (Blatchford et al., 2012). The ability to actively listen and make use of questioning, clarifying and summarising will all be useful in supporting children but they will also have a direct bearing on the relationships you have with others.

The relationship between TAs and teachers has been recognised in the research on TA effectiveness. As we suggested earlier, work with the children is enhanced when TAs, such as Sam in the case study, have sufficient time for collaborative planning and preparation with the teacher. Clearly defined roles, expectations and working practices support successful partnerships between teachers and TAs but 'successful partnerships do not just happen; they have to be worked at, redefined and renegotiated' (Goepel et al., 2015: 257). The relationship you have with your teacher can be the most challenging to establish and can be undermined if the teacher has a low perception of the TA's professional identity and feels that their own role is being threatened. We established earlier that TAs in many settings are taking more of a teaching role, which can lead to a shift in the power relationship with the teacher. According to Biggs and Cunningham (2009: 24), 'The most successful relationships between teachers and TAs are relaxed, open and based on mutual respect.' Good working relationships with teachers benefit all concerned and can give TAs confidence and empower them to seek further responsibility in their workplace.

Dunne *et al.* (2008) identified TAs as having a predominantly nurturing role and you will probably agree that you often develop this role with the pupils you support most frequently. The research into TA deployment has identified that pupils with special educational needs spend more time interacting with the TA than with the teacher. This research also recognised that their individual attention, differentiation and help with inclusion is viewed positively (Blatchford *et al.*, 2012). TAs are often in the position of supporting pupils' social and emotional needs and the interactions between TAs and pupils are often less formal than those between teachers and pupils. These interactions have been found to be more active and sustained than those with teachers (Blatchford *et al.*, 2012). The implication is that TAs' communication skills need to be of a high standard to effectively support the children with the greatest needs. We saw earlier, however, that TAs often focus on task completion and too frequently provide pupils with answers to questions rather than developing pupil thinking and independence. The skill lies in recognising when a child needs you to intervene and when they are able to function independently.

As we have just recognised, a TA will often have better knowledge of the child they work with than does the teacher. According to Blatchford *et al.* (2012: 49), 'TAs are in a strong position to act as effective mediators or "connectors" between the school and parents'. This role again makes demands on the TA's ability to communicate appropriately with parents. The SEND Code of Practice (DfE, 2015) makes frequent reference to the need to listen to parents' views and to involve them in making decisions about provision for their child. This suggests that there are a usually a number of people involved in a child's education and your ability to work well as part of this team is another key requirement of your role. Effective teamworking draws upon the interpersonal skills of the team members and requires good communication, listening, negotiation and delegation. Making the most of the skills and knowledge each member brings to the team is important. As part of a multi-agency approach to supporting a child, the TA may play an important role in communicating information about the child to other practitioners. Although you may not feel that this should be your responsibility, it is likely that you do this on a regular basis. We have established that for most, the TA role is diverse and makes many different demands, illustrated in the personal reflection above. TAs are required to be flexible, adaptable and skilled in working with others. Research by Dunne *et al.* (2008) on pupils' and TAs' perceptions listed adaptability, patience, sensitivity, empathy, approachability, supportiveness, responsiveness, attentiveness and a sense of humour as suitable attributes for TAs.

REFLECTION POINTS

■ Consider the different relationships that are part of your role in school.

■ What helps you to build productive relationships?

■ What hinders you in building productive relationships?

■ Which of the personal attributes identified above do you draw upon most frequently and which of these skills do you feel you need to develop further?

Chapter summary

This chapter has established that over the last two decades the role of the TA has changed significantly and TAs generally now have a more focussed role. There is a greater emphasis on accountability and ensuring 'value for money', which creates many challenges and puts pressure on TAs to perform well. At the same time school budgets are being cut and opportunities for training and development for TAs are further restricted.

Despite these challenges we know that TAs draw upon a number of personal skills to ensure they are meeting the needs of children with diverse needs. TAs also demonstrate their flexibility and adaptability when working with teaching staff, including other TAs, external professionals and parents.

Like you, many TAs are taking responsibility for their professional development. Some TAs are undertaking professional development to support them in their current roles and others because they aspire to become teachers in the future. Opportunities for career progression will be discussed in Chapter 14.

Although findings from research into the effectiveness of TAs vary, it is clear that TAs have become an integral part of the school workforce and have a significant part to play in the education and well-being of children and young people.

FURTHER READING

Education Endowment Fund (EEF) (2015) https://educationendowmentfoundation.org.uk/ (Accessed: 5 November 2017).

Hayes, J. (2002) *Interpersonal approaches at work.* Hove: Routledge.

MITA (2017) *Maximising the impact of teaching assistants.* Available at: http://maximisingtas.co.uk (Accessed: 2 November 2017).

Russell, A., Webster, R. and Blatchford, P. (2013) *Maximising the impact of teaching assistants.* Abingdon: Routledge.

Sharples, J., Webster, R. and Blatchford, P. (2015) *Making best use of teaching assistants: Guidance report,* Education Endowment Foundation. Available at: https://educationendowmentfoundation.org.uk/uploads/pdf/Making_best_use_of_TAs_printable.pdf.

References

Blatchford, P., Bassett, P., Brown, P., Martin, C., Russell, A. and Webster, R. (2009) *Deployment and impact of support staff.* London: Institute of Education, DCSF.

Blatchford, P., Russell, A. and Webster, R. (2012) *Reassessing the impact of teaching assistants.* Abingdon: Routledge.

Biggs, S. and Cunningham, S. (2009) *Making the most of your TA.* Abingdon: Routledge.

Cajkler, W., Tennant, G., Tiknaz, Y., Sage, R., Tucker, S. and Taylor, C. (2007) 'A systematic literature review on how training and professional development activities impact on teaching assistants' classroom practice (1988–2006)'. In: *Research Evidence in Education Library.* London: EPPI-Centre, Social Science Research Unit, Institute of Education, University of London.

Chambers, D. (2015) *Working with teaching assistants and support staff for inclusive education.* Bingley: Emerald Group Publishing Limited.

Department for Children, Schools and Families (DCSF) (2010) *Statistical First Release, School Workforce in England (including pupil: teacher ratios and pupil: adult ratios) January 2010 (provisional).* Available at: http://education.gov.uk/rsgateway/DB/SFR/s000927/sfr11-2010v2.pdf (Accessed: 15 September 2015).

Department for Education and Employment (DfEE) (1997) *Excellence for all children: meeting special educational needs.* London: DfEE.

Department for Education and Employment (DfEE) (1998) *The National Literacy Strategy: A Framework for Teaching.* London: DfEE.

Department for Education and Employment (DfEE) (1999) *The National Numeracy Strategy.* London: DfEE.

Department for Education and Skills (DfES) (2003) *Raising standards tackling workload: A National Agreement.* Available at: http://webarchive.nationalarchives.gov.uk/20130401151715/http://education.gov.uk/publications/eOrderingDownload/DfES%200172%20200MIG1975.pdf (Accessed: 2 November 2017).

Department for Education (DfE) (2015) *Special educational needs and disability code of practice: 0 to 25 years.* London: DfE.

Dunne, L., Goddard, G. and Woolhouse, C. (2008) 'Teaching Assistants' perceptions of their professional role and their experiences of doing a Foundation Degree', *Improving Schools.* Vol. 11, No. 3, pp 239–249.

Gardner, H. (1993) *Frames of Mind: the theory of multiple intelligences.* New York: Basic Books.

Goepel, J., Childerhouse, H. and Sharpe, S. (2015) *Inclusive primary teaching: a critical approach to equality and special educational needs and disability* (2nd edn). Northwich: Critical Publishing.

Goleman, D. (1996) *Working with emotional intelligence. Why it can matter more than IQ.* London: Bloomsbury.

Giangreco, M., Carter, E., Doyle, M. and Suter, J. (2010) 'Supporting students with disabilities in inclusive classrooms: Personnel and peers', in R. Rose (ed.), *Confronting obstacles to inclusion: International responses to developing inclusive schools.* Abingdon: Routledge, pp 247–263.

Higgins, H. and Gulliford, A. (2014) 'Understanding teaching assistant self-efficacy in role and in training: its susceptibility to influence'. *Educational Psychology in Practice.* Vol. 30, No. 2, pp 120–138.

Kerry, T. (2005) 'Towards a typology for conceptualizing the roles of teaching assistants'. *Educational Review.* Vol. 57, No. 3, pp 373–384.

Lamb, B. (2009) *Special educational needs and parental confidence (Lamb Inquiry),* Available at: https://education.gov.uk/publications/eOrderingDownload/01143-2009 DOM-EN.pdf (Accessed: 30 August 2015).

MITA (2017) *Maximising the Impact of Teaching Assistants.* Available at: http://maximisingtas.co.uk (Accessed: 2 November 2017).

Moyles, J. and Suschitzky, W. (1997) *Jill of all trades? Classroom assistants in Key Stage One, a report for the Association of Teachers and Lecturers.* London: ATL.

Ofsted (2002) *Teaching assistants in primary schools: an evaluation of quality and impact of their work.* London: Ofsted.

Russell, A., Webster, R. and Blatchford, P. (2013) *Maximising the impact of teaching assistants.* Abingdon: Routledge.

Sharples, J., Webster, R. and Blatchford, P. (2015) *Making best use of teaching assistants: Guidance report.* London: Education Endowment Fund.

Walton, A. and Goddard, G. (eds) (2013) *Supporting every child: a course book for foundation degrees in teaching and supporting learning* (2nd edn). London: Learning Matters.

2

Education policy

Cheryl Hedges

CHAPTER OVERVIEW AND AIMS

- To consider the history, role and function of education

- To identify ways in which the activities of TAs are framed by educational policy

- To enable the reader to reflect and engage with ideological differences in educational policy

- To understand that the development of the curriculum and assessment is not a neutral phenomenon

- To understand that pedagogy is a political issue

Introduction

This chapter considers a very limited area of educational policy: curriculum and assessment; pedagogy; and the organisation and structure of schools, beginning with a historical overview. This chapter will encourage a more critical under-standing of educational policy and to accept the importance of political debate in shaping the future of educational policy, to improve young people's experiences. This critical thinking will support you in informing your practice and encouraging reflection and analysis of educational beliefs and practices, in order to reflect on the purpose and function of education at all levels, from the curriculum we offer children, to the way we assess and compartmentalise them. Cunningham (2012) argues strongly that it is the 'world beyond the classroom' that determines the world of the primary school and that 'the context of primary teaching is innately political' (2012: 1). The policy debate will inform your understanding of other areas discussed in this text, for example the approaches to curriculum content in Chapter 5 and also the support for children with special educational needs and disabilities (SEND) in Chapter 10.

These two views of education expressed by Jaspal and Ben, who are practising TAs, are shared by some educators:

'I am not interested in politics: I just want to do my best for the kids.'

'Children need to be able to get jobs and young people need to leave school with good qualifications that employers want and mean something, and the government needs to make sure that this happens.'

The role of government and the function of education is one that has always been central to educational provision in England since the introduction of compulsory education with the 1870 Foster Education Act. The role of education either for individual fulfilment or for producing workers with the appropriate skills is a debate that continues today. For some, education is a means of role allocation and selection, a contributor to a meritocracy. Boronski and Hassan (2015: 47) offer an accessible summary of these approaches outlining a functionalist view of education being a neutral and fair system that uses scientific, effective measures such as tests and examinations to select for employment and training. This view of education is one which believes education serves the interests of society and must produce individuals who fulfil economic functions. Educational policy thus serves to ensure that this prerequisite is fulfilled.

What is educational policy?

Educational policy has many interpretations. It is used to describe activities at national and governmental levels, what Ball (2017: 10) describes as 'big P' policy, as well as policy at the school or institutional level, where policy is enacted and described by Ball as 'small p' policy. Both these interpretations of educational policy will be explored. The 'big P' interpretation describes the laws passed by parliament, e.g. the Education Reform of Act of 1988 which introduced standard attainment tests (SATs), and the direction and guidance of the Department for Education (DfE). Some people argue that schools have become political footballs and that education should be excluded from the political debate. Ball (2017: 3) states that politicisation is linked to the belief that the purpose and function of education is to produce an effective and skilled labour force. The nature and structure of education in England has always been subject to political values and social expectations. The focus here is on the educational policies of England, as other parts of the United Kingdom have historically different political systems and are not subject to the legislative process of the Westminster parliament. For example, the National Curriculum is a requirement for English maintained schools only, with the Scottish and Welsh governments retaining powers to establish their own curriculum as well as other areas of educational policy such as university tuition fees. These differences are discussed in Chapter 5.

REFLECTION POINTS

■ Reflect on children in your setting. Do you think they get a good deal from the current curriculum and schooling? How would you change things for the better for these children?

■ Which of the statements from Jaspal and Ben above do you most agree with? Why?

■ What do you think about politics and education?

■ Which view of education do you agree with? Can you think of examples to support either of the functions of education discussed above? 'small p' or 'big P' (Ball, 2017: 10)

Ideology of education

You may have heard colleagues suggesting that education has become too political and schools should be left alone to teach. Many teachers also believe that politicians use schools for their own ideological purpose. For much of the history of formal education in England, teachers and local authorities, or local education authorities in the post-war era, were responsible for curriculum and policy. However, the origins of a national education system were politically motivated. The introduction of compulsory schooling and state intervention were established by the 1870 Education Act. Many Acts were to follow, which mainly focused on the school-leaving age but left curriculum, pedagogy and even school organisations in the hands of local providers such as local education boards or churches. The 1944 Education Act, known as the Butler Act, introduced free secondary education for all children. The provision was on the basis of selection by examination to determine the education they should receive: academic education at the grammar school along with the secondary modern school for those children who would work in manual occupations and technical schools for those who would benefit from technical or vocational training. This Act also introduced one compulsory subject to be studied in schools: religious education (RE). RE remained the only subject to be compulsory in schools for the next 40 years.

The debate around the ideological origins of education is well documented in many texts, including Ball (2017), and is subject to ideological interference. An ideology is a set of ideas that inform and give coherence to practice (Meighan and Siraj-Blatchford, 1997). Bartlett and Burton (2016: 22) offer the following definition of ideology: 'Systems of broad beliefs and values about the nature of the world are termed ideologies'. Some consider that education has relatively recently become 'politicised' and that there was a time when politics did not interfere in the work of educators, schools or pedagogy. However, that may not be the case. The establishment of a free compulsory education system has its origins in the nineteenth century, via the 1870 Education Act, which introduced for the first time the notion that the state (government) had responsibility for the provision of education. This was the beginning of educational policy. The introduction of free compulsory education up until the age of ten was not smooth and was fraught with ideological conflict regarding the purpose and function of education and the impact on the social and political world. Some argued that it would benefit the developing industrial economy as there would be an improvement in productivity, due to increased levels of literacy and numeracy. Others believed that the education of the masses could lead to an overthrow of the current political establishment. Although we now know that the latter did not occur, this debate continues to drive current policy tensions and many will agree that 'Since the 1980s education has been in a perpetual state of reform' (Forrester and Garratt, 2016: 11).

Policy is an important aspect of understanding schools and education. Our working day is determined by educational and government policy: from the subjects we teach (the National Curriculum was introduced in 1988), the support for pupils (via the SEND Code of Practice 2014), the make-up of the workforce, the structure of the school, the name of the school, e.g. community school, technology college, academy and free school, to the internal governance of the school (Ball, 2017: 5–6). According to Forrester and Garratt (2016: 3), even the government department with responsibility for education has evolved over the last 20 years from one that has sought to incorporate every aspect of a child's education, including the Every Child Matters agenda, known in 2007 as the Department for Children, Schools and Families (DCSF) to one with a refocus on teaching, known as the Department for Education (DfE) from 2010.

Curriculum and assessment

It is difficult to do credit to the discussion of curriculum and assessment at both secondary and primary level, so it will be considered in a thematic way. A strong theme is the centralisation of control of the curriculum, as demonstrated by the introduction of the National Curriculum in the 1988 Education Reform Act. The second theme is one of the development of competition and marketisation of education since the Thatcher governments of the 1980s to the present day. This offered a very distinct flavour to the politicisation of education once described as neoliberalism and neoconservatism. Adams (2014) provides us with a coherent overview of this debate explaining that neoliberalism emphasises minimum intervention in school matters, the creation of competition between schools to raise standards, schools controlling their own finances and parents having the information such as examination results to allow them to make an informed choice of school for their children. Neoconservatism emphasises traditional behaviour, values and standards.

We take for granted the National Curriculum and the government prescription of what children should learn, but this has not always been the case. Kelly (2013) (cited in Allen and Ainley, 2013) offers a good description of the development of primary curriculum within the context of the neoliberal agenda of the 1980s, arguing that the curriculum has become more narrow with a focus on basic skills in maths and English and the measurement of success or failure by the end of Key Stage 2 tests. Children increasingly are limited in their experiences of art, drama and sport. The National Curriculum has undergone many reforms, the most recent in 2013. At secondary school, subject choice is already predetermined, with little opportunity to study vocational or arts subjects. Most children are required to study the English Baccalaureate subjects of mathematics, English, science, modern foreign languages (MFL) and history or geography. See Chapter 5 for more on the structure and ideology of the school curriculum.

CASE STUDY 2.1

Yvonne

I find my work as a TA has become harder over the years and I am more and more involved in targeted and interventionist activities with one child or small groups of children. When I first started in my role I was a general assistant in the classroom working with the teacher and all the children in that class. I really enjoyed the variety and the relationship I had with the classroom teacher. I learnt so much about teaching and how children learn. Now I hardly see the teacher and I am expected to produce the material for my group and assess and monitor their performance. We have to report weekly to the year co-ordinator and feed back on progress. I feel like the school has become an exam factory. I used to want to become a teacher but now I am not so sure. I know

(continued)

(continued)

my role is now funded by pupil premium money and the school must show how this money is being used and spent. Children on free school meals (FSM) don't do very well in education and I understand that we should be improving their performance but schools are only part of a child's life and some of them in my school have very troubled and poor backgrounds and we need to do more to help them socially. It seems like teachers don't have any control over how they teach any more. I am also worried that some teachers are only thinking about children in terms of how well they do in the SATs exams and forget that they are only children. Most of the teachers are at the school for 8.00am and don't leave until 6.00pm every day.

ACTIVITY

■ What are the things that frustrate Yvonne in her role?

■ Which of these things can you relate to current political ideology?

As we established in Chapter 1, the role of TAs in schools has always been a varied one and this is acknowledged by Yvonne in the case study above. It was originally mostly focused on the support of the class teacher or one-to-one support for an individual child. This focus however has diversified for a number of reasons: firstly the increasing pressure on schools to demonstrate 'impact' of all spending and interventions on a child's academic progress; secondly, the 'financial accountability agenda' that discusses education in the context of a neoliberal agenda of 'value for money', 'performativity' (Ball, 2017) and accountability. There is currently a significant tension, according to Kelly (2013) between a focus on the well-being of the child and the content of the National Curriculum. The contradictions of the Plowden Report (1967), the National Curriculum (2013) and the previous Every Child Matters agenda of the last Labour government all conspire to create a situation in schools where TAs find themselves being pulled in different directions.

The origins of a national curriculum can be traced back to the 1970s, to what is now seen as a significant crossroads for education: the Ruskin College Speech (1976) of then Labour Prime Minister James Callaghan. The debate centred on the purpose and function of education. The central themes of the debate were to suggest that the 'progressive' education policies of the 1960s, such as the idea of child-centred learning set out in the Plowden report (1967), had failed. The 1970s saw increased levels of unemployment and in particular youth unemployment. The political analysis of the day was that these high levels of youth unemployment were the result of poor educational performance and a failure of education to meet the needs of the economy and employers. These themes were to become the central pillars of Conservative educational policy of the 1980s onwards until today. This ideological position has been described as neoliberalism and neo-conservativism, terms which were introduced above and the discussion of curriculum has for the last 30 years been located within these two theoretical frameworks. Neoliberalism emphasises the economic function of education seen for example in the requirement of schools to produce students who are needed by the labour market. Neo-conservativism focuses on the traditional aspects of curriculum, seen for example in the teaching of history where there is a focus on British history, in particular the English kings and queens, and rote learning. This is epitomised in the beliefs of Michael Gove, Secretary of State for Education 2010–2015, something that even Simon Schama, esteemed historian and advisor to Michael Gove began to question by 2013 (Rahim, 2013).

Another consequence of the introduction of the National Curriculum in 1988 was the centralisation and standardisation of subject knowledge. The most significant change to the National Curriculum under the Labour government in 2003 was the focus on not just the knowledge that children should learn but how teachers should teach this knowledge. This was prescribed in the national Literacy and Numeracy Strategies. School timetables were essentially written by the Secretary of State for Education, so that all children would receive the same menu of teaching across the country. To the neoliberals (those who believe that education should serve the needs of the economy and the national interest) this was important in maintaining standards. These standards are in competition with other countries as displayed in the international league tables of the Programme for International Student Assessment (PISA).

REFLECTION POINTS

■ Think about the curriculum in your setting. What would you change or keep if you were in charge of the school curriculum?

■ How do you support the curriculum in your role as a TA?

■ How has the role of the TA in supporting the curriculum changed over the last five years, either from your own experience or by surveying the views of other more experienced TAs in your setting?

Organisation and structure of schools

Today we take for granted that all children receive free education and are expected to remain in some form of education up until the age of 18 (Raising Participation Age, 2006 Education Act). However, a historical overview illustrates that education has been subject to social change and political pressure. The most significant piece of educational policy was the 1944 Education Act introduced by Butler, a Liberal peer. A central pillar of the 1944 Education Act was the notion that intelligence is an inherited and measurable attribute. The tripartite education system selected children at the age of 11 through the 11+ examination which determined the secondary education received according to supposed 'intellectual abilities' determined by the exam. A pass grade resulted in attendance at a grammar school with a focus on academic learning, but to fail was to be allocated to a secondary modern school, where you would be given a diet of vocational learning which was deeply gendered.

This tripartite system increasingly came under pressure from research suggesting that the 11+ examination was not reliable and was severely limiting the academic success of the children who had been labelled failures. By the mid-1960s comprehensive schools, which did not select by ability, were becoming the norm and the government issued an instruction to abolish the discredited grammar schools in favour of community comprehensive schools.

We now have a diversity of educational providers: academies, both independent and those that are part of multi-academy trusts (MATs), as well as free schools, foundation schools and community schools. This process has been accelerated since 2011 and the Importance of Teaching Education Act, first under the former Coalition government and more recently the Conservative government. The process has been ostensibly under the 'democratisation and choice' banner, but the consequences have been to privatise educational provision by reducing the power and authority of local authorities and encouraging the 'academisation' of the English school system. This marketisation of education is well discussed in Ball (2017), and Harvey (2005) offers a historical and political overview of the ideology of neoliberalism that has driven these educational reforms from the 1970s onwards.

CASE STUDY 2.2

Chris

I enjoyed school but I always felt I was a bit 'thick'. I didn't pass the examination to go to grammar school so went to the local comprehensive with my friends and older brother and sister. The school was good but I never got into the top set, where you got all the best teachers. I think I was in the bottom set for most subjects and I wasn't expected to do well at school. I left school at 16 with very few qualifications, mainly Certificates of Secondary Education (CSEs) and no O Levels (pre-1988 qualifications for 16-year-olds). I became a hairdresser by accident as my aunty had a business, so I worked with her and did my qualifications at the local college. It was only after I had my own kids that I started to think again. I began reading more and developed an interest in psychology and criminology, initially from watching television and then doing research of my own, and getting books out of the local library and charity shops. I began to find the world of books more interesting than cutting hair. When my kids did their GCSEs I decided to return to college and do my GCSE English at the college. It was amazing. I gained a grade B! It was then I decided to apply to do an Access course at the college focussing on social sciences as I couldn't find a course just for psychology. It all began to make sense. I suddenly had a motivation to study. I applied to study criminology at a local university, being encouraged to do so by my college tutor. I am now coming to the end of my first year and I absolutely love it. It sometimes makes me sad to think that I was labelled a failure at 11 but I might never have found criminology had I taken the 'normal' route.

REFLECTION POINTS

- Make a list of the different types of school that you have knowledge or have experience of. Put them into a chronological order, of when they opened.

- Describe each of the types of schools/institutions in terms of their organisational characteristics. For example, who appoints the headteacher? What is the relationship with the local authority?

- Do you think that Chris's experience continues today?

Pedagogy

Pedagogy refers to the way teachers teach and children learn. Classrooms were the domain of teachers and it was accepted that their professional knowledge and understanding would guide their practice. This was the state of affairs up until the late 1970s and the period between the 1950s and 1970s was seen as a 'Golden Age' (Whitty, 2008). The period was characterised by local education authority (LEA) control of schools and teachers designed and implemented their own curriculum. There were examinations at 16, some of which were set and marked by teachers. At primary school there was increasing interest in a more child-centred approach or 'progressive' educational philosophy. This approach rejected the idea that children should sit in rows and receive didactic instruction from the knowledgeable teacher at the front of the class, as was the norm in the Victorian era. The new philosophy began to see children as individuals, with their own pace of learning and interests. The Plowden Report (1967) formalised these ideas and challenged the view that children's intelligence could be identified by a test at the age of 11. This educational policy was very much influenced by the psychological thinking of Piaget, Vygotsky and earlier philosophers of education such as Dewey. You will find out more about these views in Chapter 4. With progressive education, the emphasis was on individual development with 'the needs and interests of the learner being central. The learning process is seen as vital with discovery and experimentation being at its heart. Learning is held to be rewarding in itself and pupils/students maintain high motivation because of this' (Bartlett and Burton, 2016: 26).

This teaching and learning experience had the most influence in primary schools, with the organisation of learning in groups, a focus on learning through play, children developing at their own pace and a more formative approach to assessment. Schooling was seen as a way that children could learn about their own needs and abilities and fulfil their own dreams. Government policy increasingly began to question these ideas and by the 1970s a narrower and more structured approach to learning and teaching was once again emerging for the reasons discussed above.

REFLECTION POINTS

- Can you identify examples of these traditional and progressive philosophies from your own practice and setting?

- Can you think of any difficulties that adopting either of these approaches might have on the organisation of schooling?

- Do you think we should once again allow teachers to make all the decisions around pedagogy, curriculum and standards?

Chapter summary

This chapter has introduced you to the idea that education is not neutral but is the product of political processes, with the government increasing its power and authority over schools in the last 30 years. Philosophy and ideology have also been considered as a means of making sense of educational practices.

FURTHER READING

Allen, M. and Ainley, P. (eds) (2013) *Education beyond the coalition: reclaiming the agenda*. London: Radical Books.

Bartlett, S. and Burton, D. (2016) *Introduction to education studies* (4th edn). London: Sage.

References

Adams, P. (2014) *Policy and education.* Abington: Routledge.

Ball, S. (2017) *The education debate.* Bristol: Policy Press.

Bartlett, S. and Burton, D. (2016) *Introduction to education studies* (4th edn). London: Sage.

Boronski, T. and Hassan, N. (2015) *Sociology of education.* London: Sage.

Cunningham, P. (2012) *Politics and the primary teacher.* London: Routledge.

Forrester, G. and Garratt, D. (2016) *Education policy unravelled.* London: Bloomsbury.

Harvey, D. (2005) *A brief history of neoliberalism.* Oxford: Oxford University Press.

Meighan, R. and Siraj-Blatchford, I. (1997) cited in P. Adams (2014) *Policy and education.* New York: Routledge.

Rahim, S. (2013) 'Simon Schama on Michael Gove', *The Telegraph.* Available at: http://telegraph.co.uk/culture/books/10146897/Simon-Schama-on-Michael-Gove.html (Accessed: 16 October 2017).

Whitty, G. (2008) 'Changing modes of teacher professionalism: traditional, managerial, collaborative and democratic', in B. Cunningham, *Exploring professionalism.* London: Institute of Education, Bedford Way Papers, pp 28–49.

3 Reflecting on learning

Becoming a student in higher education

Clare Bright

CHAPTER OVERVIEW AND AIMS

■ To explore what it is to be a student in higher education

■ To understand the nature and demands of studying and learning

■ To encourage reflection

■ To suggest strategies and resources for effective independent learning

Introduction

The decision to go to university is a significant step for most and can bring many challenges. This chapter has been written to support your decision to study for a Foundation Degree and to help you understand the demands of studying and learning in higher education. You will be introduced to ideas about learning and encouraged to reflect on the factors that can impact on your studies. The skills required for effective learning will be identified and you will be signposted to resources to support the development of these key skills. We hope that whatever stage you are at in your learning journey, you will find some of the ideas discussed in this chapter useful.

Becoming a student in higher education

To begin we will reflect on your motivation for studying for a Foundation Degree. In the light of the research that has recently been carried out on TA deployment it may be that you have been asked to change your working practices or to take on a different role in your setting. You may be driven by the desire to be more informed so you can do your job well or because ultimately you want to become a teacher. You may be curious to learn more about teaching and learning or even want to challenge yourself in an academic context. Whatever the reason for embarking on this personal 'journey' there are some important ideas that you will need to think about so you can make the most of this new opportunity.

Research by Dunne, Goddard and Woolhouse in 2008 found that many TAs have been out of education for a number of years and as a consequence need to develop the skills to study at higher education level. They can, therefore, lack confidence in their own skills and abilities. Here are some comments from TAs just starting their Foundation Degree . . .

'Am I clever enough?'

'Will I be brave enough to speak out in the sessions?'

'I haven't written an essay for years – I don't know how to any more.'

'Will anyone be interested in what I have to say?'

'Will I get help?'

'Will my brain be able to cope at this age?'

'How will I be able to find the time to do all this reading?'

Many of you will feel anxious but also excited about the decision you have made. Some of these comments may sound very familiar and echo your own thoughts as you embark on your degree. Read the following reflection from Kathryn, at the time a TA in a primary setting, as she recalls the day she started her Foundation Degree.

CASE STUDY 3.1

Kathryn

It was an important day for me and one which I had been looking forward to for a long time. I was excited about finally going to university, but nervous about the level of academic writing that would be required; the amount of personal study the course would involve; how I would find the time in my already busy schedule to fit that commitment in; and of course, quite concerned that I had never written to the standard that I thought would be expected. When I first started I didn't really know what I was capable of as a student in higher education or what I would need to do to be successful at it.

(continued)

(continued)

I quickly realised that my fellow students had their own worries, some of which were similar to mine, and that what brought us all together was a genuine interest in benefitting as much as possible from our time at university. Whenever we struggled to maintain focus on our studies, or we felt challenged, either by our tutors, by our circumstances or by our own study choices, we knew we could turn to each other for advice. We regularly drew on each other's valuable and collective experiences of working in education to support and motivate one another to reach our goals.

Receiving feedback on my assignments was quite difficult in the early days and reading back through my reflective journal, it seems I was feeling quite dejected by the response to my first efforts. Over time I began to realise that constructive criticism from my tutors and peers could be a positive part of the learning process. I soon learned how to combine this feedback with self-reflection to deepen my learning and make real progress towards becoming an independent, self-reflective practitioner.

REFLECTION POINTS

- What are your own feelings on beginning your learning in higher education?

- What skills do you already have that will support your studies?

- What skills and attributes do you think you need to develop in order to learn successfully at this level?

- What are going to be your greatest challenges?

- How are you going to overcome these? What will you need to do to help overcome these?

Becoming a learner in higher education

You may well have some preconceived ideas about becoming a university student and what this will involve. Many new students worry that they will not be clever enough to study at this level so it might be useful to explore a few ideas around intelligence and what it is. Traditionally it has been accepted that intelligence is measurable, the commonly known measure being the IQ test. Highly intelligent people have a high IQ but does this mean they are clever at everything? An intelligence test only measures what can be measured and yet the characteristics of intelligent people include things like creativity, abstract thought, intuition and inventiveness, which are much harder to measure.

In Chapter 1 we introduced Howard Gardner's theory of multiple intelligences (1983) which suggests that there are several intelligences that we possess in different degrees. You might be aware that you are particularly good at relating to others or you might have good musical or physical skills. Gardner's theory acknowledges that our culture and experiences are significant in determining our different intelligences. For example you might have been encouraged to learn to play a musical instrument as a child or to engage in puzzles and games with your family. For others these were not part of growing up and have therefore not been developed to the same degree. The important point is that we can develop our skills and intelligences and learn new ones, provided we are given opportunities to do so in a way that suits how we learn. This will be explored in more depth later in this chapter.

Working hard, meeting deadlines, working independently, managing studies along with work and family life, studying, reading, note-taking, writing and discussing ideas might be some of the activities you associate with being a student. We do not deny that all these are important and at the end of the chapter we provide a number of recommended texts and links to useful resources to support you in acquiring these study skills. However, according to Wingate (2006), learning is rather more problematic than this and she has recognised that higher education offers the opportunity to 'promote other aspects of students' growth as people.' We suggest that becoming a successful student in higher education requires adopting the characteristics of a learner and a 'student identity' rather than just a set of skills.

We are keen to explore with you the complexity of learning at university and to consider the view that we should be equipping students to engage with what some call 'troublesome knowledge' (MacDougall and Trotman, 2009: 21). To do this, 'it is therefore necessary to teach students that knowledge is constantly developing, and that they are expected to question existing knowledge and contribute to its development, using evidence from previous contributors' (Wingate, 2006: 463).

In order to help you to develop these skills we need to consider ideas around being curious, creative and imaginative and being prepared to grapple with difficult concepts that challenge what you thought you understood! Bolton (2010: 70) has discussed the idea of being 'open to uncertainty about learning needs and possibilities' and she suggests three foundations for students to take control of their learning, which are:

- certain uncertainty – seeing 'not knowing' as a positive and allowing it to open up new possibilities

- serious playfulness – a willingness to explore and unearth something new

- unquestioning questioning – being prepared to actively enquire.

Bolton believes that by adopting these foundations we can find out about ourselves and feel more able to discover different selves. For this to happen we need to be in safe educational environments where we feel confident to take risks (Bolton, 2010). At this point it would be helpful to remember that you are likely to already have knowledge and understanding gained from previous experiences of studying and working. You may be feeling that these are irrelevant or unimportant but they will underpin your studies and you need to use them to give you confidence as you take on new learning.

Look at how you answered the first reflective question, which has probably revealed some of your insecurities about becoming a student. The ability to overcome self-doubt and to embrace ambiguity takes time and practice. Mindset theory can help us to understand why it can sometimes be so difficult to persevere with something challenging. The work of Carol Dweck has revealed that success and failure can be influenced by having either a fixed or growth mindset (Dweck, 2006). Having a fixed mindset means that challenges are avoided because failure suggests a lack of ability which acts as a barrier to learning. On the other hand, having a growth mindset encourages effort as it is viewed as worthwhile. Receiving feedback is seen as supporting improvement rather than revealing limitations and will support learning. This links to Kathryn's words earlier when she acknowledged that feedback became an important part of her development. At this point it would be useful to reflect on your own response to feedback and consider if you have a growth mindset.

How do you learn?

To support you in developing the skills that are required to study in higher education it is helpful to understand how you learn. Learning is a complex process that involves a number of different interactions and is improved by creating the right conditions for learning that will vary between individuals. Discussions on how we learn often begin with looking at 'learning styles' and yet we must exercise caution when deciding if we have a particular style of learning. You may be familiar with the terms visual, auditory and kinaesthetic (VAK) learning which were adopted by many schools about fifteen years ago. It was thought that it was necessary to know children's preferred learning styles in order to teach them in a way that would maximise their learning. This approach was adapted from research into the brains of people with brain injuries but subsequent reviews of this research found serious limitations and raised concerns around the use of VAK in the classroom. These concerns remain and it is considered far more helpful to see learning as a set of skills and attributes rather than as a particular style.

We can refer back again to Howard Gardner's multiple intelligence theory which has established that we have a range of intelligences which are developed to different levels, dependent on experiences and circumstances. Knowing our strengths can help us to identify our preferences for learning and how we process information effectively. With this knowledge we might adopt different strategies that promote learning. For example, you might like to use images and mindmaps to help you to retain information or you might prefer to record information on your phone. You might be most productive working in a quiet environment or you might have a messy workspace that fires your imagination.

REFLECTION POINTS

■ What are your learning preferences?

■ How do you create the right conditions for your learning?

■ How do you respond to feedback?

■ Are your responses helpful and how might you ensure that you learn from feedback?

Deep and surface learning

The idea of deep and surface learning was first discussed in a paper by Marton and Säljö in 1976. They identified different approaches that students took when asked to read an article that they would later be questioned on. The study found that some students memorised sections of information which Marton and Säljö termed the 'surface approach'. Other students searched for the underlying concerns, implications and meanings within the article. Marton and Säljö termed this the 'deep approach'. These students were more able to answer the questions; they had a better understanding of the article and could recall the messages within it. Subsequent studies have had similar results and have contributed to the overall conclusion that students who take a deep approach have higher-quality learning outcomes.

The two approaches discussed above are characterised by particular actions that lead to different levels of engagement with knowledge. These are detailed below:

Deep approach to learning

■ An intention to understand material for oneself

■ Vigorous and critical interaction with knowledge content

■ Relating ideas to one's previous knowledge and experience

- Discovering and using organising principles to integrate ideas

- Relating evidence to conclusions

- Examining the logic of arguments

Surface approach to learning

- An intention simply to reproduce parts of the content

- Ideas and information are accepted passively

- Concentrating only on what is required for assessment

- Not reflecting on purpose or strategies

- Memorising facts and procedures routinely

- Failing to distinguish guiding principles or patterns

Reflecting on these characteristics we can see some correlation with the three foundations proposed by Bolton (2010). Although there have been accusations that the terms 'deep' and 'surfac' learning are too simplistic and judgmental they should not be perceived as static or fixed. Studies have shown that students do change their approach according to the differing demands presented by different tasks. A third category of learner described by Säljö, is the strategic learner, characterised by the desire to achieve the highest grades possible. A strategic learner will choose strategies that enable efficient time management and learning which might sometimes compromise depth of understanding of the material.

Bloom's taxonomy

This is sometimes described as a measurement tool for thinking. It represents, in pyramidal form, a hierarchy of skills for learning that become progressively more complex. It was first conceived in the 1950s by Benjamin Bloom and revised in the 1990s. As a learner acquires the skills associated with each level they become more able to engage in higher-order thinking. Looking back at the activities associated with a deep approach to learning we can see some similarities between the two.

Factors that impact on learning

There are many things that impact on our ability to learn and we look at some of them below.

Motivation

We have discussed different approaches to learning and these relate strongly to levels of motivation. We might be extrinsically motivated by the need to achieve high grades in order to progress in a particular career or our motivation might be driven intrinsically by the desire to prove something to ourselves or others.

A useful model that we can refer to is Maslow's Hierarchy of Need which was proposed by Abraham Maslow in the 1940s to recognise how people are motivated by levels of need. Reflecting on your own learning, you will no doubt agree that it difficult to concentrate if you have physiological needs – if you are cold, hungry or tired. If these needs are met, the theory proposes that we need to feel safe and secure in order to learn. As each level of need is satisfied and the barriers to learning removed, the theory suggests that we are more likely to be able to engage with learning to reach our potential (cited in Robins, 2012). If you apply Maslow's theory to your own circumstances you might be able to identify any potential barriers to your own learning and this may help you to understand why your learning is sometimes ineffective.

Constructivism and social constructivism

These ideas about learning are based on the key principle that learning is an active process. The learning theory put forward by Lev Vygotsky (1962) is known as constructivist theory and suggests that people construct their own understanding and knowledge of the world through experiencing things and reflecting on those experiences. Vygotsky proposed that by working with a 'more knowledgeable other' we can move our learning through a 'Zone of Proximal Development' (ZPD) to reach our learning potential. By interacting with others we can be supported to reach new levels of learning. This is clearly a key factor in Kathryn's learning as a student in Higher Education as she refers to the support and motivation she gained from working with others.

Reflection

According to Moon (2004: 80) 'Reflection is part of learning and thinking. We reflect in order to learn something, or we learn as a result of reflecting, and the term "reflective learning" emphasises the intention to learn from current or prior experience.' To support your learning you are often encouraged to engage in reflection and it can be helpful to use a model of reflection to help you. One such model is Gibb's Reflective Cycle (1988) which leads you through a series of six stages from a description of the event, recognition of feelings, an evaluation, analysis and conclusion to an action plan. It is worth remembering to acknowledge the positive emotions and events as well as the negative ones. A criticism of Gibb's model is that it can be carried out quite superficially.

Another model that is commonly used is Kolb's Learning Cycle (1984) which can help us to learn from our experiences by taking us through four stages. Stage three, named 'abstract conceptualisation' asks us to generate a hypothesis about the meaning of our experiences. Stage four is 'active experimentation' where we 'test' the hypotheses we have recognised. The key to this model is the active engagement with the stages to enable effective reflection. For more detail on models of reflection please see the reference to the Jennifer Moon text in the Further Reading at the end of this chapter.

Developing the habit of reflection is recognised by Cottrell (2013) who suggests that student performance can be improved by reflecting on how you learn. She encourages you to consider your motivation, attitudes, study strategies and blocks to learning, amongst other things. There are ways of recording your reflections that might inspire you to make a habit of reflection. One suggestion is to keep a learning journal in which you can record your thoughts, ideas and emotions as you progress through the course. This can be a useful way to clarify things and to see how you are managing your learning and how you tackle difficulties. Keeping this private can allow you to record honestly how things are going. There are some risks to engaging in honest reflection as an in-depth examination of events can reveal some aspects that are challenging and that feel unsurmountable. However, by looking at something from multiple perspectives it hoped that different ways forward can be found.

Study skills

We mentioned earlier in this chapter that study skills are important in order to become an efficient and effective learner. For you as a student in higher education, the skills that you will be using on a daily basis are numerous but the most useful ones are described below.

Time management and planning

This is often one of the most challenging aspects for students who, like you, might have multiple commitments as well as now having to find additional time to study. Understanding how you use your time is important because poor time management can cause additional stress and anxiety. There are many strategies to help you make more productive use of your time and becoming efficient at other study skills such as reading and note-taking can save you considerable time.

Reading

This is an interesting skill to reflect upon because obviously you are able to read but how effective is your reading? We read in different ways for many different purposes and whilst studying for your degree you will be required to read a range of different sources such as academic texts, journal articles, online resources and policy documents. There are numerous strategies to help you to read efficiently but most important of all is to ensure that you are reading appropriate material and that you understand what you are reading.

Note-taking

This is a skill that will help you to manage all the information that you need to access now that you are studying. You will be required to make notes both from your reading and from taught sessions. There are several different styles of note-taking such as linear and pattern notes and mind-maps. You might use a variety depending on the situation and the reason for making the notes. Whatever style you prefer to use it is vital that your notes are easy to access and to understand.

Academic writing

As Bedford and Wilson (2013: 75) suggest, success on your degree course will depend to a great extent on the quality of the written work you produce. You will be expected to write in a style that you are not accustomed to, following certain conventions that will seem odd at first. The ability to articulate well- informed, critical discussions is challenging but this will become easier with practice. There is a wealth of advice available to help you manage the process of structuring and writing an academic assignment.

Searching for literature

Knowing how to use your university library will be very important for accessing much of the information you need but you will also need to locate electronic resources. You may think that this will be easy as we are so used to using search engines to find all sorts of information in our daily lives. However, to find accurate, high-quality, academic sources you will need to learn to plan and refine your search strategies. Time and effort can be wasted if you do not learn how to do this efficiently.

Referencing

This is an essential but time-consuming activity. Having located appropriate sources to inform your work it is vital that you accurately record where all your information is from. Not to do so puts you at risk of plagiarism which is 'the intentional or unintentional use of another person's work as if it were your own' (Bedford and Wilson, 2013: 113) and is a serious academic offence. Most cases of plagiarism are unintentional and are a result of poor referencing. Familiarise yourself with the referencing style that you are required to use at your university and allow yourself plenty of time to do your referencing. It is surprising how long it can take.

Working with others

As we have already discussed in this chapter, working with friends on your course is usually very beneficial to your learning. Sometimes however, you are put in a position of having to work with people you do not know which can be more stressful, particularly if this is for an assessed or presentation or collaborative project. In Chapter 1 we looked at some of the interpersonal skills you will have developed in your role at work and it is likely that you will draw on these to support effective group work at university. Being skilled in communication, negotiation, delegation, co-operating, encouraging and supporting will enable you to become an effective group member.

We acknowledge that there is not enough space here to discuss these skills in depth so we are providing you with a number of links to resources and strategies to help you to develop them further (see below). You will also find that your own university will have many resources to support your studies, so do find the time to become familiar with these.

Box of Ideas – http://boxofideas.org/ideas/practical-skills-in-education/further-ed/study-skills/

LearnHigher Resources – http://learnhigher.ac.uk – ready-made materials on a range of key study skills topics

Open University Resources – http://open.edu/openlearn/skills-for-study – tips and guidance on effective study

Palgrave study skills – https://he.palgrave.com/page/study-skills/

Skills You Need – https://skillsyouneed.com/learn/study-skills

Unilearning – http://unilearning.uow.edu.au/main.html

Chapter summary

In this chapter we have asked you to reflect on your motivation to study at university and we have discussed some of the concerns that are common for those of you returning to academic study after a break. The characteristics of being a student have been identified and we have established that you will need to develop a wide range of skills to help you make the most of university and to be successful in your studies. This chapter has introduced you to some different ideas about learning and to some of the factors that can influence your ability to learn. We have recognised how taking time to reflect on your learning can be a powerful way to identify your learning preferences and to see ways to overcome difficulties. The value of working with others has also been discussed. We hope this chapter has given you some insight into the requirements of studying in higher education and that it has equipped you with some ideas on how you can become a confident and successful student.

FURTHER READING

Moon, J. (2004) *Reflection in learning and professional development, theory and practice.* Abingdon: RoutledgeFalmer.

Richie, C. and Thomas, P. (2014) *Successful study* (2nd edn). Abingdon: Routledge.

Stella Cottrell has written a number of books that will support your studies. She has written about critical thinking, essay writing and study skills.

Tony Buzan has written in particular on memory techniques and mind-mapping.

References

Bedford, D. and Wilson, E. (2013) *Study skills for foundation degrees* (2nd edn). Abingdon: Routledge.

Bloom, B.S. (ed.) (1956) *Taxonomy of educational objectives: the classification of educational goals: handbook I, cognitive domain.* New York: Longmans, Green.

Bolton, G. (2010) *Reflective practice* (3rd edn). London: Sage.

Cottrell, S. (2013) *The study skills handbook.* Basingstoke: Palgrave Macmillan.

Dunne, L., Goddard, G. and Woolhouse, C. (2008) 'Starting a foundation degree: teaching assistants' self-perceptions of their personal and professional identities' *38th Annual SCUTREA Conference*, 2–4 July 2008, University of Edinburgh, available at http://leeds.ac.uk/educol/documents/172310.pdf.

Dweck, C. (2006) *Mindset: how you can fulfil your potential.* New York: Random House.

Gardner, H. (1983) *Frames of Mind: the theory of multiple intelligences.* New York: Basic Books.

Gibbs, G. (1988) *Learning by doing: a guide to teaching and learning methods.* London: Further Education Unit.

Kolb, D. (1984) *Experiential learning: experience as a source of learning and development.* Englewood Cliffs, NJ: Prentice-Hall.

Marton, F. and Säljö, R. (1976) 'On qualitative differences in learning: 1: outcome and process'. *British Journal of Educational Psychology.* Vol. 46, pp 4–11.

McDougall, J. and Trotman, D. (2009) 'Doing theory on education', in S. Warren (ed.), *An introduction to education studies: the student guide to themes and contexts*. London: Continuum, pp 13–23.

Moon, J. (2004) *A handbook of reflective and experiential learning*. Abingdon: Routledge Falmer.

Robins, G. (2012) *Praise, motivation and the child*. Abingdon: Routledge.

Vygotsky, L.S. (1962) *Thought and language*. Cambridge, MA: M.I.T. Press.

Wingate, U. (2006) 'Doing away with study skills'. *Teaching in Higher Education*. Vol. 11, No. 4, October, pp 457–469.

PART II
Curriculum issues

The developing child

Jane Beniston

CHAPTER OVERVIEW AND AIMS

■ To develop your understanding of the importance of child development

■ To consider different areas of child development

■ To promote the use of holistic approaches to the developing child

Introduction

This chapter will introduce you to key elements of child development and the importance of using theoretical models to support children's learning and development. It will consider different areas of development including language, cognition, social and emotional issues. The chapter will conclude by focussing on the importance of supporting children's holistic development.

What is child development?

Child development is studied on all courses that consider children at the heart of their learning. Doherty and Hughes (2009: 4) define child development as the 'study of change'. Humans go through the developmental stages of pre-natal, post-natal, childhood, adolescence and finally adulthood. Throughout these stages changes are not random but usually follow a typical human pattern. We can consider three specific areas of development: human growth; maturation (which involves biology and genes); and learning (which is based on experiences and is a process).

Theoretical perspectives

An understanding of child development is based upon theoretical underpinning, but we need to understand what we mean by theory and how theory is helpful to us in our work with children and young people. The English word 'theory' was derived from a technical term in Ancient Greek philosophy. The word *theoria* meant looking at, viewing or beholding, and refers to contemplation or speculation, as opposed to action. This is where the concept of putting theory into practice is crucial to our work. Theories are used to make sense of our world, to explain and predict phenomena. Theories are not fact, however, and must not be treated as such. You must be careful when dealing with false assumptions, which are often called fallacies. Theories come about from two distinctive lines of reasoning: inductive, where a researcher notices patterns and creates a theory, and deductive, where a research makes a theory and then studies that area to prove or disprove the theory. There are many different theories within the field of child development, some of which will be considered within this chapter.

Physical development

Developmental change results from an interaction between biology (nature) and experience (nurture) called epigenesis. This interaction is complex, but overrides the need for a nature/nurture debate around development. Environmental factors (nurture) can directly influence biological growth (brain growth) and genetic factors influence the environment (a sociable child will produce a different response from that of a reserved or anti-social child). There is a new field of study within development called epigenetics that explains how expressions of genes are modified by environmental factors.

Lindon (2005: 115) considers why physical development is important to other areas of development. Progress in physical growth and development makes new behaviours possible and determines potential experiences. Skills in physical development support co-operative play, building muscle strength, lung capacity and bone density. It is also crucial for managing body control for reading and writing later in life. Physical growth which may not follow the norm also affects the responses of others to the child and can affect a child's self-esteem.

In early physical development babies are very dependent upon their carers to bring them things of interest. As they develop physically they are able to explore more of their environment. Goddard Blythe (2004) describes the first building blocks for later learning linked to physical development as the first ABC: A = attention; B = balance; and C = co-ordination.

Physical growth and development do not proceed randomly but follow a particular pattern.

Cephalocaudal growth occurs in a head-to-toe direction, and proximodistal development occurs from the centre of the body outwards, e.g. control over the neck and head before hands and feet. Predictable patterns of physical development continue after birth. From 0 to 2 years there is rapid physical development. From 2 to 6 years physical and cognitive abilities are extended; in which children learn about the world and their own capabilities. From 6 to 11 years physical growth slows, whilst movement skills are consolidated and there is preparation for puberty (Doherty and Hughes, 2009). Pre-natal and post-natal growth and development can by affected by genes and the environment. Within the womb these factors are called teratogens. Teratogens can adversely affect the health, development and growth of the unborn child. Some of the teratogens are: drugs (prescription and non-prescription drugs), alcohol, tobacco and infectious diseases. The health and well-being of the mother can also affect the unborn child.

Physical movement skills fit into two categories: fine motor (small movement, usually with hand) and gross motor (larger movements of the body). As muscular development increases, children practise and refine all of these movements. There are three main perspectives around motor development. The first, advocated by Gesell (1928), is a biological approach where the sequence of development is controlled by process of maturation. The environment (nurture) has a supportive role but development is controlled by genes (nature). The second puts forward the idea of development as an information-processing model, in which information about movements is interpreted and codified by the brain then acted upon by comparing new information with memory. The final approach considers an ecological perspective, supported by Haywood and Getchell (2009). Movement skills evolve from initial attempts to fully automated and consistent mastery. They conclude that there are stages defining specific and sequential motor behaviours. This approach stresses the importance of environment (nurture). A child's development cannot be separated from the context of that child. As practitioners we must consider the context, culture and environment of the child when observing development. Gallahue and Ozmun (1982) also outline four key phases of motor development:

- Reflexive movement phase (First movement/reflexes)

- Rudimentary movement phase (0–2 years)

- Fundamental movement phase (2–7 years)

- Specialised movement phase (7 years – puberty)

Language development

Early studies of language development were based around keeping detailed dia-
ries of children's speech which produced longitudinal studies but generalisations
were often made from small and biased samples. Charles Darwin and Jean Piaget
used this diary method to record their children's development. Developments in
technology allowed for the use of tape recorders to document children's speech,
but this did not allow for the nuances of meaning. Video recording and tests are the
main research techniques used today. There are three main theories of language
development: Learning theory, Nativist theory and Interactionist theory.

Learning theory is based upon a behaviourist approach where children are seen
to learn language through reinforcement and operant conditioning. Developed
through the work of Skinner (1957), this theory suggests that children use and
copy language and they are rewarded by responses when the language used is
appropriate. This theory could be described as an environmental or nurturing
theory of development. This theory does not allow for the fact that children say
things they could not possibly have heard, however, such as mouses, rather than
mice. It also does not explain children's ability to use complex language at such
an early age.

The Nativist theory suggests that language is innate and introduces a language
acquisition device (LAD), developed by Chomsky (1968). This theory explores
the nature or biological /genetic theory of development. Critics state that there is
no neurological evidence as yet, however, for this theory. Also if this is an innate
ability why does it take so long for us to acquire the rules of grammar?

The final theory of language development discussed within this chapter stresses
the significance of the interplay between environmental and biological factors,
sometimes called epigenesis. The interactionist theory developed by Bruner (1983)
suggests that parents provide children with a language acquisition support system
(LASS). The use of the high-pitched voice – often called motherese – and the idea

of scaffolding children's language development are the keys to this idea of a support system. There are also criticisms of this theory, however, as no account is taken of cultural norms with families – i.e. some parents do not provide feedback to children but children still acquire language.

It is useful here to consider how bilingual or multilingual children acquire languages. In the early stages of life, children's brains are able to learn words in one or more languages quickly and to switch between these languages. There are many cognitive advantages to learning a language at an early age, including synapse development. (This is explained further in Chapter 13.)

Stages or sequences of language development follow a similar pattern across cultures, from the pre-linguistic stage at 0–12 months (of cooing, vocal play and babbling) to the emergence of first words between 1 and 2 years of age. This stage is often called a naming explosion and includes holophrases in which single words represent a whole sentence. By the age of 2–3 years, sentences appear in the form of telegraphic speech in which key words are used. From 3 years onwards children develop more vocabulary and the use of questioning.

Cognitive development

Cognition entails thinking, reasoning and problem solving which also involves levels of metacognition: thinking about thinking (Doherty and Hughes, 2009). These processes are electrical pulses between brain neurons or cells. Jean Piaget (1953), a Swiss psychologist, considered that cognitive development was the result of an interaction between an individual and the environment. Piaget's developmental theories have been widely used in education and are often seen as the most dominant in terms of cognition development theory. They are based on the idea that the developing child builds cognitive structures in the brain that increase with the child's development. Piaget sees a definite, inevitable sequence of maturational steps starting with biological mechanisms and culminating in a highly developed system of abstract operations. There are four distinct stages within this theory: sensory motor, pre-operational, concrete operations and formal operations. The child comes to terms with their surroundings by organising activities into schemata by the process of assimilation and accommodation. Creating these schemata was seen by Piaget as a process by which the child is an active participant in the concept learning process. Key terminology associated with Piaget is: Assimilation (which describes how new information is fitted into existing schema), Accommodation (when existing schemas are modified to fit in the new information), Equilibrium (which is achieved when the new knowledge matches the child's current schema, and dis-equilibrium which occurs when new information does not match or fit in with the child's current schema).

In contrast with Piaget, Vygotsky (1962) saw knowledge as being imparted by a more experienced person, although he also believed that children should be active learners. Vygotsky also stressed the importance of context and culture in children's learning. He considered that children are born with innate natural unlearned capacities, which he termed elementary mental functions. Other non-human animals have elementary mental functions, but Vygotsky thought that it was through social interaction that we develop language and then we are able to develop higher mental functions. Vygotsky developed what could be called a stage theory, as did Piaget. The stages through which every child had to pass, however, within Vygotsky's model ages were not as rigid. He placed much more emphasis on the role of experience in concept formation than did Piaget.

Key terminology related to Vygotsky's theories are the Zone of Actual Development (ZAD) where the actual development is the level a child reaches independently and potential development is the level a child reaches through assistance of adult guidance or from a more able peer, and the Zone of Proximal development (ZPD) which is the difference between actual and potential level of development.

Activities that are planned within the child's ZPD stimulate learning. Closely linked to this theory is the theory of 'scaffolding' or 'guided participation', developed by Bruner (1983). Scaffolding or guided participation are adult behaviours that support the learning during the learning process. A study by Wood (1998) concerning how children were supported and scaffolded by their mothers provided a description of five different levels of support:

- general verbal encouragement

- specific verbal instructions

- indicates requirements

- prepares for activity

- demonstrates

Bruner (1960) also developed a theory of cognitive growth. His approach (in contrast with Piaget's) looked to environmental and experiential factors. He considered learning to be an active process in which learners construct new ideas or concepts, based upon their current/past knowledge. He considered the idea that the curriculum should be organised in a spiral manner, so that children continually build upon what they have already learnt. This is a useful model to develop within the classroom or setting. Bruner (1960) also developed a theory of cognition, but this is not seen as a stage theory. There are three parts that make up Bruner's theory:

- enactive representation, in which a baby learns to control its body and how to act physically upon the environment, e.g. this can be likened to muscle memory when we first learn how to crawl, walk, then run. (This is encoded in our muscles and is evident when we learn a new skill such as driving or touch-typing.)

- iconic representation i.e. from the age of 1, a child employs mental images, which are primarily visual or otherwise senses-based

- symbolic representation; by means of language, reasoning and other systems of meaning. A child passes through these representations for each concept learnt. To gain deep learning a child needs the enactive concrete examples before moving through the iconic to a more symbolic representation.

REFLECTION POINTS

- When you are in conversation with children, how do you support their language development? What strategies do you use? Does this differ depending on who you are talking with? Why?

- Think of an activity you did recently with a child or group of children. How did you scaffold their learning?

- Consider each theorist in turn: are their ideas/theories evident in your practice?

- How could you use these theories to support children's learning and development?

Emotional, social and moral development

By six months of age most emotions have been seen in young babies and are usually expressed through facial expressions, behaviour and verbal responses. The first expressions are that of startle, distress and disgust, followed by anger, surprise, interest and sadness. Fear is one of the last emotions to develop. Expression of emotions can be supported through positive relationships which can be developed through secure attachments.

Attachment is a bond of affection between two people in which a sense of personal security and commitment is bound up within that relationship. Secure attachment is seen as crucial to healthy early development. One of the key theorists around attachment is John Bowlby. Bowlby (1958) developed a theory around the relationship between the caregiver and the child, which he termed an attachment relationship. He linked this theory with ideas around bonding and the impact of this relationship. Ainsworth (1973) also contributed to ideas around attachment and noted that children use adults as a secure base and safe haven from which they explore their environment. In early years settings, Elfer *et al.* (2003) advocate the key person approach. The key person can provide:

- a sense of security and continuity for the child

- a 'special' relationship with the child

- understanding and knowledge of the child

- individual planning for the family

- support for the mother or main carer

- a close physical presence to the child during the settling-in period

- a close relationship with the family to sustain connections with home.

Emotional literacy is concerned with developing an emotional vocabulary, linked to emotional intelligence. Daniel Goleman (1995) developed the idea of emotional intelligence and its five stages.

There are five stages of emotional intelligence according to Goleman (1995):

1. knowing your own emotions
2. managing emotions
3. motivating yourself
4. recognising emotions in others
5. handling relationships.

Emotional regulation and emotional intelligence are vital skills children need to be able to function successfully in everyday life. The development of this emotional regulation is, in the first instance, dependent on the behaviour of the caregiver towards the infant. It is, therefore, crucial that the child develops warm and positive relationships with caregivers at home and within the educational settings they attend.

Social development begins with the child acquiring a sense of self, linking to ideas of self-concept and self-esteem. A sense of self is not achieved in a single step; as we grow and develop we learn more about ourselves. How we describe ourselves to others changes as we get older. The development of self is not a constant process; some aspects of self remain the same for years, while others change rapidly. A sense of self is a cultural construction. In some communities individual uniqueness is seen as vulgar and uncivilised, as is independence, since the needs of the group outweigh the needs of the individual and likewise consideration of self is seen as selfish. Charles Horton Cooley put forward a theory of the 'looking glass self'. He stated that other people's views build, change and maintain our self-image. This theory considers the interaction between how we see ourselves and how others see us. What we see in the mirror is ourselves, but this is based on what other people think of us. George Herbert Mead proposed another slightly different theory of self. He sees self as a combination of 'I' (subject) and 'Me' (object). 'I' is the pure awareness and 'Me' are the things about myself of which 'I' am aware. Rogers' (1961) theory is probably the most well-known theory regarding 'Self' as the central ingredient. He described the self as a social product which develops out of interpersonal relationships and strives for consistency. Rogers (1961) identifies a basic human need for positive regard from others and from oneself; where this positive regard is received a child will develop a positive self-concept, but where positive regard is not received it can case psychological ill-health and inner conflict. According to Lawrence (1996: 1) 'Self-concept is best defined as the sum total of an individual's physical characteristics and their evaluation of them.' The ideal self is seen as the type of person we would like to be. If there is a large gap between how we see ourselves and our ideal self we tend to have low levels of self-esteem.

REFLECTION POINTS

- Do you have a key person approach?

- How do you develop and promote positive relationships and attachment with children?

- How do you demonstrate positive regard to the children and members of staff with whom you work?

- How do you develop children's self-esteem in your setting?

Schaffer (1996) sees moral development as 'a set of principles or ideals that help the individual distinguish right from wrong and to act on this distinction'. Piaget (1932) proposed that moral behaviour and moral reasoning develop in two identifiable stages called 'heteronomous morality' and 'autonomous morality'. Heteronomous morality occurs for children aged between 3 and 7–8 years of age. Piaget (1932) states that these children believe rules are fixed and unchallenged. They can see the difference between intentional and unintentional outcomes, but base their judgement on the severity of the outcome. They are unable to see alternative interpretations, which take motives into account. Autonomous morality concerns children over 8 years of age who begin to learn that rules can be changed by experiment and trial and error. The motive or intention of action is taken into account and the punishment is viewed as more related to the offence. Piaget used stories to investigate and define these age-related stages. Kohlberg (1985) identified three stages of moral development: pre-conventional (aged 6–13); conventional (aged 13–16); and post-conventional (aged 16–20+). Eisenberg (2000) also offers a model of moral development; but, instead of exploring wrongdoing and punishment, he explored self-interest against the possibility of helping someone else. Eisenberg proposed a model of pre-social reasoning with five levels.

Holistic development

Considering holistic development means that each area of development is dependent on the other. All areas must be considered in a holistic way to ensure children develop to their full potential. Although development is described with different areas (physical, social, emotional, language and cognitive), each area connects in order for the child to develop. A holistic way of thinking seeks to encompass and integrate multiple layers of meaning and experience, rather than defining human possibilities narrowly. Through play, the holistic development of the child is encouraged.

The holistic development approach also needs to consider children in their environment. As stated earlier, a child's development cannot be separated from the context of that child. From the 1970s, Urie Bronfenbrenner worked to describe the impact of environment on children. His theory is sometimes known as the ecological systems theory. This theory is a reminder that children do not develop in isolation. The theory emphasises the complexity of everyday life. Bronfenbrenner (1979) refers to a perspective in which the child is viewed within the model of a 'system within a system'. According to Bronfenbrenner (1979), there are five systems which guide human development, behaviour and interaction: the microsystem (the system that has the most impact on the child and includes family, school, neighborhood and peers); the mesosystem (the connections between the microsystems, including interactions between the peers, family and teachers); the exosystem (the wider social settings that support the child and family); the macrosystem (the cultural context of the child including ideology, laws and customs); and the chronosystem (which is involves the element of time and changes over time).

From this theory we must remember that each child is unique and therefore so is his/her system.

Chapter summary

This chapter discusses child development, its key elements and the importance of using theoretical models to support children's learning and development.

A wide range of key theoretical perspectives have been outlined to introduce the concepts of physical development, language development, cognitive development, and emotional, social and moral development. The chapter concludes by focussing on the importance of supporting children's holistic development.

FURTHER READING

Doherty, J. and Hughes, M. (2009) *Child development theory and practice 0–11*. Essex: Pearson Education Limited.

Keenan, T., Evans, S. and Crowley, K. (2016) *An introduction to child development.* London: Sage.

Lindon, J. (2005) *Understanding child development: linking theory and practice.* Oxford: Hodder Arnold.

References

Ainsworth, M.D. (1973) 'The development of infant-mother attachment', in B. Caldwell and H. Ricciuti (eds), *Review of child development research*. Vol 3. Chicago: University of Chicago Press.

Bowlby, J. (1958) 'The nature of the child's tie to his mother'. *International Journal of Psychoanalytic*. Vol. 39, pp 350–373.

Bronfenbrenner, U. (1979) *The ecology of human development: experiments by nature and design*. Cambridge, MA: Harvard University Press.

Bruner, J. (1960) *The process of education*. Cambridge, MA: Harvard University Press.

Bruner, J. (1983) *Child's talk: learning to use language*. Oxford: Oxford University Press.

Chomsky, N. (1968) *Language and mind*. New York: Harcourt Brace Jovanovich.

Cooley, C.H. (1902) *Human nature and the social order*. New York: Scribner.

Doherty, J. and Hughes, M. (2009) *Child development theory and practice 0–11*. Harlow, Essex: Pearson Education Limited.

Eisenberg, N. (2000) 'Emotion, regulation and moral development'. *Annual Review of Psychology*. Vol. 51, pp 665–697.

Elfer, P., Goldschmied, E. and Selleck, D. (2003) *Key persons in the nursery: building relationships for quality provision*. London: David Fulton.

Gallahue, D. and Ozmun, J.C. (1982) *Understanding motor development*. Dubuque, IA: Brown & Benchmark.

Gesell, A. (1928) *Infancy and human growth*. New York: Macmillan.

Goddard Blythe, S. (2004) *The well balanced child: movement and early learning*. Stroud: Hawthorn Press.

Goleman, D. (1995) *Emotional intelligence: why it can matter more than IQ*. London: Bloomsbury.

Haywood, K. and Getchell, N. (2009) *Life span motor development*. Leeds: Human Kinetics.

Kohlberg, L. (1985) *The psychology of moral development*. San Francisco, CA: Harper & Row.

Lawrence, D. (1996) *Enhancing self-esteem in the classroom* (2nd edn). London: Paul Chapman Publishing.

Lindon, J. (2005) *Understanding child development linking theory and practice.* Oxford: Hodder Arnold.

Mead, G.H. (1913) 'The social self'. *Journal of Philosophy, Psychology and Scientific Methods.* Vol. 10, pp 374–380.

Piaget, J. (1932) *The moral judgement of the child.* New York: Harcourt Brace.

Piaget, J. (1953) *The language and thought of the child.* London: Routledge.

Rogers, C. (1961) *On becoming a person.* Boston: Houghton Mifflin.

Schaffer, H. (1996) *Social development.* Cambridge, MA: Blackwell.

Skinner, B. (1957) *Verbal behaviour.* New York: Appleton Century Crofts.

Vygotsky, L. (1962) *Thought and language.* Cambridge, MA: MIT Press.

Wood, D. (1998) *How children think and learn.* Oxford: Blackwell Publishing.

5 Curriculum development and approaches

Clare Bright and Cheryl Hedges

CHAPTER OVERVIEW AND AIMS

■ To support the reader to undertake a reflective and critical review of recent developments in the curriculum

■ To consider the formation of the curriculum and curriculum design

■ To consider the curriculum as experienced by the children in their settings

■ To discuss the concepts of creativity and imagination

■ To explore the approaches to the way in which curriculum is enacted

---

Introduction

This chapter will introduce you to some of the philosophies which form the foundation of curriculum design and practice. Throughout the chapter you will be encouraged to reflect on your own experience and practice in regard to the way the curriculum is experienced by children and young people in your setting. We will also explore the ways in which creativity and imagination can enhance professional practice and learning. We will draw on a range of perspectives and illustrate with reference to examples of innovative practice in a range of different settings.

Context

When we discuss curriculum we are referring to the policy as applied to English schools, and we have to remember that the curriculum of Northern Ireland, Scotland

and Wales is a devolved matter. It is difficult to recall a time before we had government control of the curriculum through the National Curriculum, which was introduced in England in 1988. Previous to this the only curriculum expectation included in law was the teaching of religious education which was enshrined in the 1944 Butler Education Act. The National Curriculum was the cornerstone of the 1988 Education Reform Act which, amongst other things, set national standards and benchmarks for attainment in the form of Standard Assessment Tests (SATs), set expectations for subject content and introduced the inspection framework of the Office for Standards in Education (Ofsted). Subjects were divided into core subjects – English, maths and science and Foundation subjects.

The primary curriculum

During the 1970s and 80s there was a distinct shift at primary level away from the child-centred, topic-based approach that had been recognised by a number of educationalists of the time such as Mary Plowden in her report of 1967. Primary school timetables began to replicate those of a secondary school where subjects had their discrete allocated time slot and there was little opportunity to break down the subject boundaries. Over the next 30 years the National Curriculum was reviewed to reflect the policy agenda of the government at the time: their ideologies, priorities and philosophies.

The original aims of the National Curriculum were to create a more consistent approach to curriculum delivery and student entitlement. It was designed to enable schools to be compared more easily with one another. There was considerable resistance to this as teachers were worried that the overly prescriptive and detailed subject content would shift the emphasis onto 'teaching to the test' (Wyse et al., 2013: 21). It needs to be remembered, however, that the National Curriculum had never been about how to teach but what to teach, although this has been forgotten by teachers, who over the years have come to see the National Curriculum as undermining their professional identity. To some extent this was reinforced by the widespread adoption of the Qualifications and Curriculum Authority (QCA) schemes of work that were produced in 2000. Many teachers fell into the trap of delivering these prescriptive lesson plans and began to believe that these were the National Curriculum, although they were never statutory. This was seen as detrimental to teachers taking a creative and flexible approach to teaching and learning.

Following a review in 2000, the National Curriculum was slimmed down, although teachers still felt it was overcrowded. In 2009 Sir Jim Rose, commissioned by the 2005 Labour government, proposed a curriculum based around areas of learning similar to those of the Early Years Foundation Stage (EYFS) (DfES, 2008). This 'simplification of the curriculum' (Wyse et al., 2013: 24) had it been implemented, would have reduced the emphasis on discrete subject teaching and encouraged a more integrated approach to teaching and learning at the primary level. At the same time a wide-ranging independent review of primary education conducted by Robin Alexander from Cambridge University was taking place. This research concluded that a change in emphasis was needed and, although not implemented, the report suggested structuring the curriculum through domains of knowledge, skill, enquiry and disposition – which again indicated that there was dissatisfaction with the current curriculum design.

Subsequent to these reviews, in 2010 the Coalition government set out to reform the National Curriculum. After a period of consultation, Michael Gove, Education Secretary at the time, promised a curriculum 'that would provide children with an introduction to the essential knowledge they would need to be educated citizens' (DfE, 2013: 6). Despite the input of a number of educationalists, Gove ignored their recommendations and decided to follow ideas taken from a number of countries such as Singapore, USA and Finland. According to Gove, the National Curriculum of 2014 assured the 'centrality of academic knowledge in the education available to all' (Gove, 2014), thus emphasising the current focus we now have in our curriculum.

The secondary curriculum

Unlike the primary school curriculum, there is a long history of a subject-defined approach. The secondary curriculum is defined by the National Curriculum and is purposively linked to perceived social, economic needs. The secondary curriculum is characterised by a number of differences from that of the primary curriculum; firstly, there has always been subject demarcation; secondly, there has been a vocational and academic divide particularly at Key Stages 4 and 5; thirdly, there has been a marked division along lines of gender and the continued existence of the hidden curriculum; finally, the secondary curriculum has more recently been moulded by successive Secretaries of State for Education by the use of performance measures. Some have argued that this has had a negative impact for children and young people by narrowing the curriculum considerably.

The timetable and the curriculum offer has been the same in England since the introduction of compulsory schooling and according to Wrigley (2014) would be recognisable to any teacher today. The curriculum at secondary level was formulated along the lines of the existing public school system for those attending grammar schools following the 1944 Education Act. As Wrigley (2014) states, the school system as established in 1870 was not intended to offer a liberal education, but rather to provide workers with the necessary skills to maintain economic growth and competition with the emerging superpower, Germany. This leads onto the second aspect of the secondary curriculum and that is the vocational and academic divide. The 1944 Act, though to be welcomed for the introduction of free secondary education, established a divide in educational provision at secondary level along the lines of academic content versus vocational provision.

The Norwood Committee (1943) distinguished between:

The pupil who is interested in learning for its own sake. . . the pupil whose interests and abilities lie markedly in the field of applied science or applied art. . . [and finally, the pupil who] deals more easily with concrete things than with ideas.

(cited in Wrigley 2014: 8).

As we identified in Chapter 2, the academic curriculum was to be taught to those who passed the 11+ and attended grammar schools (20% of children approximately). Those who failed the 11+ attended secondary modern schools which were for those young people who were likely to go on to complete manual jobs at various levels of skill. The subjects taught reflected the needs of their future occupational roles. For boys, these subjects included metalwork, woodwork and technical drawing, whereas for girls it was domestic science, typing and office practice. It is not until the late 1960s and early 1970s that examinations were introduced for those attending secondary modern schools. Those attending grammar schools often stayed on until age 16 and completed O Level qualifications; then some would complete A Levels in the sixth form, either to gain entrance to university or into non-manual clerical jobs, which were still predominantly white-collar while women continued to be associated with secretarial work. This functional relationship of school to occupational and role allocation is a central feature of functionalist theory of education and the work of Davis and Moore (1967) in particular. In addition, education was characterised by a vocational and academic divide, vocational education being the subject with the least status. The introduction of the National Curriculum in 1988 could be said to have undermined both the gender inequality and the vocational academic divide, as all children would now study the same subjects and schools would be judged and allocated a position in league tables on the performance of the children in GCSEs and SATs. This new National Curriculum was also to have a positive impact on girls' academic performance, as all children would now contribute to the league tables of schools, and expectations of girls had gradually been increasing throughout the 1970s and 80s. By the 1980s, as a result of the activism of many feminist educators and teachers, girls were no longer underachieving in education but there continued to be a difference in subject choices among boys and girls which continues today, to create a gendered labour market: hairdressers continue to be mainly women and plumbers mainly men.

There have been many attempts to develop the secondary curriculum. The Tomlinson Review suggested creating an upper secondary phase and there was the unsuccessful introduction of a range of Diplomas to eventually replace GCSEs and A Levels. Curriculum 2000 encouraged the breadth of curriculum at AS and A Level. Had the Tomlinson Review been accepted, Bartlett and Burton (2015: 138) argue it would have 'radically changed the face of 14–19 curricula and qualifications'.

The curriculum in Scotland and Wales

As previously mentioned the National Curriculum pertains only to England. Considering the close proximity of Wales and Scotland, it is interesting to recognise the distinctive nature of the curriculum they each choose to follow.

Teaching and learning in Scotland is guided by the Curriculum for Excellence (The Scottish Government, 2008) which is a non-statutory framework that started in 2008 and applies to learners from age 3 to 18. Learning is organised within four capacities and these aim to enable children and young people to become 'successful learners, confident individuals, responsible citizens and effective contributors'. There is a strong emphasis on personalisation, choice and learners' needs. There are eight curriculum areas, within which there are suggested 'experiences and outcomes', but schools and teachers are able to make decisions about what is taught and how learning is delivered. Interdisciplinary teaching is encouraged which requires clear and relevant links across the curriculum to encourage deeper, more meaningful learning.

Prior to its devolvement from England in 1998, Wales was required to follow the National Curriculum. After 1998 there came a staged implementation of the School Curriculum for Wales (Welsh Assembly Government, 2008). The approach was framed under seven core aims which were developed from the United Nations Convention on the Rights of the Child. It was seen as fairly radical to have an approach based on children's rights and was significantly different to the 'top-down' approach taken in England (Wyse *et al.*, 2013: 36). A new curriculum for Wales is due to be available in September 2018 which promises more freedom for teachers and is designed to equip young people for life.

CASE STUDY 5.1

Lyndsay

Lyndsay wants to be an interior designer when she leaves school. At 14 she already has work experience in property development with her uncle at weekends. She helps select, paint and order furnishings for his properties, which he lets. She really enjoys the

(continued)

(continued)

creativity and practical experience. She would like to study painting and decorating at college, like her uncle did when he was at school, but the school no longer offers this option. She chooses art but there is nothing in the other 'blocks' she wants to study; but the school says all students must study either history or geography and a modern foreign language. She struggles with writing and has a difficult relationship with the French department.

She speaks to her head of year and art teacher to discuss other options. They offer to discuss the possibility of college with the deputy headteacher for curriculum, but say she should agree to improve her behaviour in French classes and not get excluded from lessons.

REFLECTION POINTS

■ Compare the ideologies of the different curricula above. What are the key differences between them?

■ How is the curriculum on offer in her setting affecting Lyndsay in the case study above?

■ How could the setting meet Lyndsay's needs more effectively?

■ At what point do you think children and young people should begin to select their own curriculum or subjects to be studied?

Creativity

Ask a few people to define creativity and it is likely you will get several different responses. Creativity is often described as a 'slippery concept' because of the difficulty defining it. It is often assumed to be related to the creative arts and creative people are seen to be those who have a talent for art, music, dance or drama. This view is highly contested as creative activity is something we can all engage in and it is possible to promote creativity in all aspects of the curriculum.

In 1999 the National Advisory Committee on Creative and Cultural Education (NACCCE) provided a definition for creativity in their report *All Our Futures: Creativity, Culture* – 'Imaginative activity fashioned so as to produce outcomes that are both original and of value' (NACCCE, 1999: 30).

Imagination is often cited as a key element of creativity but even this is open to interpretation. Craft (2000: 3) refers to it as 'possibility thinking' and sees it as the heart of creativity based on asking questions. There is, however, an argument that the precise definition of creativity is not needed and that it should be viewed as a number of skills, aptitudes and dispositions. You will find many lists of characteristics of creativity which will have some variation but there will also be many similarities.

ACTIVITY

■ Write your own list of characteristics of creativity and ask a colleague to do so. Compare your lists.

You have probably included ideas such as using imagination, problem solving, risk taking, experimenting, playing, trial and error, exploring and questioning. There will be some aspects that you may not have considered such as the idea of resilience. Children who are developing their ideas should be encouraged to take risks and they therefore need to be prepared that some things might go wrong. Perseverance and resilience are essential attributes to cope with setbacks (Claxton, 2001).

The characteristics identified above can only flourish in an environment that accepts learner autonomy and allows time for children to engage in open-ended tasks that encourage a range of outcomes. Teachers need to have confidence and flexibility and the skills to recognise opportunities for thinking and working differently, described by Ofsted as being alert to 'happy accidents' (Ofsted, 2003). They need to adopt a range of approaches and encourage active learning that allows pupils to follow their interests and pursue their ideas.

Creativity in the curriculum

The above overview of the curriculum and its development suggests that the National Curriculum and the focus on literacy and numeracy in a rather sterile compartmentalised way have led to the denigration of creative and performance subjects. Teachers have long felt that performativity and 'high stakes testing' (Wyse *et al.*, 2013: 9) have challenged their professionalism and narrowed their repertoire of teaching skills. However, looking back it can be seen that there have always been opportunities for creative approaches to both teaching and learning within the school curriculum.

The NACCCE report mentioned above could be seen as a turning point in the promotion of creativity in education as it advocated that alongside having high standards of academic achievement, young people now needed to leave formal education able to 'adapt, see connections, innovate, communicate and work with others' (NACCCE, 1999: 13). In 2003 the document *Excellence and Enjoyment* (DfES, 2003) was published. This recognised the importance of engaging children in their learning and recognised that 'discovery, creativity and problem solving were the "cornerstones" of primary education' (Desailly, 2012: 34). It also strengthened the view that teachers could adapt the curriculum and have a greater say in what and how they taught. In 2005 resources designed to support teachers and schools that were trying to develop creativity were produced called *Creativity: Find it, Promote it* (QCA, 2005). The developments identified above indicate that there had been a growing awareness of the need to promote creativity in children and young people. This, however, was set alongside increasing pressure to achieve high standards in tests and to focus on the 'core subjects'. Schools were receiving mixed messages and have had to find their own ways to manage these different pressures.

Despite these pressures many schools recognise the benefits of taking a creative approach and say that they have a 'creative curriculum', but we need to question what this really means. Looking back at the definitions of creative teaching and learning we can question if some of the approaches implemented by schools include some of the features of creativity discussed above. Truly creative lessons will provide opportunities for learners to use their imagination, ask questions, problem solve, follow open-ended tasks and make their own choices in order to complete them. Fostering creativity often involves embracing pupils' ideas and giving them some autonomy over their learning.

These characteristics can be incorporated into any lesson but there are also specific initiatives that support a creative approach and some of these are recognised in the following section.

REFLECTION POINTS

■ What would you like to see in a curriculum?

■ Does your setting claim to have a creative curriculum? In the light of the discussion on creativity above, do you believe it is creative?

■ What are the benefits and barriers to taking a creative approach to teaching and learning?

ACTIVITY

- Compare a timetable from a Reception class to one for a Year 6 class. What are the similarities and differences?

Creative approaches to learning and teaching

Here we provide a brief insight into some approaches adopted by schools that include elements of creative teaching and learning.

Cross-curricular learning

This is a curriculum approach which seeks to overcome the compartmentalisation and individualisation of subjects by taking a theme, visit or activity through which knowledge, skills and understanding are taught. Practitioners offer a sound justification for this approach both at the academic and pedagogic level as it enables connections to be made across subjects and helps to embed learning.

CASE STUDY 5.2

Manjit

Here Manjit reflects on the value of a visit to the Black Country Museum in the West Midlands. She believes:

Cross-curricular themes are important aspects of promoting the National Curriculum and are also a very fun way for children to gain a wide range of knowledge, understanding and experiences. It can also be beneficial for practitioners when planning activities as they can use different links through each subject – with a good understanding of what children should know. When cross-curricular links are implemented in a suitable way through stimulating and motivating activities, this is when cross-curricular learning is a success.

However, at an academic level, there is a difficulty that by adopting a cross-curricular approach two issues emerge. Subjects might become diluted and some overlooked. Lessons need to be carefully planned to ensure coverage of the curriculum and to ensure pupils are making progress.

REFLECTION POINTS

■ What sort of cross-curricular opportunities does your setting offer?

■ Imagine there were no limits on resources. Construct a visit for children or young people from your setting. What subjects would you include and how would integrate the cross-curricular theme into your visit?

■ How can you ensure that the curriculum is covered effectively?

■ How do you measure pupil progress when several subjects are taught at the same time?

Outdoor learning

What do we understand by outdoor learning?

> *Learning outside the classroom is about raising achievement through an organised, powerful approach to learning in which direct experience is of prime importance. This is not only about what we learn but importantly how and where we learn.*

> DfES (2006: 3)

Outdoor learning has its origins in the European philosophy of education of the nineteenth century and the influence of Froebel. The idea that moving outside the classroom can foster learning, and improve experience and performance is supported by Arthur and Cremin (2010: 161). Outdoor learning refers to any activity or learning that takes place outside the classroom, so this can be in the untended field in a rural primary school, the local park, a visit to a museum or the local rugby club. Students have identified the value of outdoor learning in many ways and this often reflects the characteristics of creative learning and teaching discussed previously.

'Mantle of the Expert'

The Mantle of the Expert approach was invented by Professor Dorothy Heathcote at the University of Newcastle upon Tyne in the 1980s. It is a dramatic enquiry-based approach to teaching and learning in which pupils do all their curriculum work as if they are an imagined group of experts. As 'experts' such as scientists, town planners or archaeologists, the pupils engage in activities and tasks that provide them with some of the same kinds of responsibilities, problems and challenges that real experts might do in the real world. The approach calls for a change to the roles of pupils and teachers so there is a sharing of responsibility for learning outcomes. The teacher becomes more of a facilitator, bringing together different curriculum subjects. The pupils are often highly motivated by the challenges presented by the 'enterprise' they are engaged with.

Problem-based learning

Problem-based learning (PBL) originates in the teaching of medics at university level and is the means of teaching throughout degree courses at the University of Maastricht. Barrows and Tamblyn (1980) offer a good description of the approach which attempts to teach subjects which are related to real-life experiences and have no right or wrong answer. Savin-Baden (2007: 1) defines PBL as 'the notion of learning through managing problems'. The focus in PBL is on a topic or an issue. Schools have used PBL to promote independent thinking skills and creativity. Students are taught in mixed groups of abilities, and sometimes year groups, with teachers team-teaching across a number of disciplines. This encourages teamwork, independent thinking and positions the teacher as a facilitator rather than the possessor of knowledge.

Philosophy for children

This is an approach that enables children to learn through dialogue and the exploration of ideas, and is acknowledged to have begun in the work of Professor Matthew Lipman who opened the Institute for the Advancement of Philosophy for Children in 1974. Lipman's method of learning through collaborative enquiry helps children realise that they do not always have to have the right answers (something that is all too frequently expected in conventional learning and teaching), but they gain the confidence to ask questions and learn through discussion. They learn to value others' views and they develop the confidence to express their own ideas. The approach gives all children a voice and develops a number of skills including independence, imagination, listening and reasoning.

Chapter summary

In this chapter we have presented an overview of how the curriculum in both primary and secondary settings has developed. This recognises that the curriculum has changed according to the government of the time and the ideas they have about learning and what they believe children should know and understand. We have found that sometimes these ideas are in conflict with teachers' knowledge of their pupils' needs. We have looked at definitions of creativity and established that it is a difficult concept to define and that there are a number of characteristics of creative teaching and learning. There is a need for teachers to acknowledge the benefits of fostering creativity and to find ways to promote it in the classroom despite the pressures on them for pupil progress and attainment. Successful schools are able to achieve these through a creative curriculum that develops both pupils' skills and knowledge. We have provided an overview of some common creative approaches that recognise the characteristics of creativity and contribute to innovative ways for pupils to learn.

FURTHER READING

Mantle of the Expert (2017) Available at: http://mantleoftheexpert.com/ (Accessed: 17 October 2017).

Philosophy for Children (2017) Available at: http://philosophy4children.co.uk/ (Accessed: 17 October 2017).

Claxton, G. (2017) *Building Learning Power.* Available at: https://buildinglearningpower.com/ (Accessed: 17 October 2017).

Ofsted (2010) *Learning: Creative approaches that raise standards.* Available at: http://creativity cultureeducation.org/wp-content/uploads/learning-creative-approaches-that-raise-standards-250.pdf (Accessed: 17 October 2017).

References

Alexander, R. (2008) *Dialogic teaching* (4th edn). York: Dialogos.

Arthur, J. and Cremin, T. (2010) *Learning to teach in the primary school.* Abingdon: Routledge.

Bartlett, S. and Burton, D. (2015) *Introduction to education studies.* London: Sage.

Barrows, H. and Tamblyn, R. (1980) *Problem based learning: an approach to medial education.* New York: Springer Publishing.

Central Advisory Council for Education (1967) *Children and their primary schools (The Plowden Report).* London: HMSO.

Claxton, G. (2001) *Wise up: learning to live the learning life.* Stafford: Network Educational Press Ltd.

Craft, A. (2000) *Creativity across the primary curriculum.* London: Routledge.

Davis, K. and Moore, W.E. (1967) 'Some principles of stratification', in R. Bendix and S.M. Lipset (eds), *Class, status and power.* London: Kegan Paul.

Department for Education and Skills (DfES) (2003) *Excellence and enjoyment: a strategy for primary schools.* London: DfES.

Department for Education and Skills (DfES) (2006) *Learning outside the classroom manifesto.* Nottingham: DfES Publications.

Department for Children, Schools and Families (DCSF) (2008) *Statutory framework for the early years foundation stage.* Nottingham: DCSF Publications.

Department for Education (DfE) (2013) *The national curriculum in England.* Available at: http://gov.uk/dfe/nationalcurriculum (Accessed: 17 October 2017).

Desailly, J. (2012) *Creativity in the primary classroom.* London: Sage.

Education Scotland (n.d.) *What is curriculum for excellence?* Available at: https://education.gov.scot/scottish-education-system/policy-for-scottish-education/policy-drivers/cfe-(building-from-the-statement-appendix-incl-btc1-5)/What%20is%20Curriculum%20for%20Excellence? (Accessed: 17 October 2017).

Gove, M. (2014) *The future of vocational education*, speech at McLaren, 3 March 2014.

Learning Wales (n.d.) *Curriculum.* Available at: http://learning.gov.wales/resources/improvementareas/curriculum/?lang=en (Accessed: 17 October 2017).

National Advisory Committee on Creative and Cultural Education (NACCCE) (1999) *All our futures: creativity, culture and education*. London: DfEE.

Ofsted (2003) *Expecting the unexpected: developing creativity in primary and secondary school*. HMI 1612.

Ofsted (2008) *Learning outside the classroom: how far should you go?* Available at: http://dera.ioe.ac.uk/id/eprint/9253 (Accessed: 17 October 2017).

Qualifications and Curriculum Authority (2005) *Creativity: Find it, promote it! – promoting pupils' creative thinking and behaviour across the curriculum at Key Stages 1, 2 and 3 – practical materials for schools*. London: QCA.

Savin-Baden, M. (2007) *A practical guide to problem-based learning online*. London: Routledge.

The Scottish Government (2008) *Curriculum for excellence*. Available at: http://scotland.gov.uk (Accessed: 31 October 2017).

Welsh Assembly Government (2008) *Framework for children's learning for 3 to 7-year-olds in Wales*. Available at: http://ibe.unesco.org/curricula/unitedkingdom/wlk_pp_lpr_fw_2008_eng.pdf (Accessed: 31 October 2017).

Wrigley, T. (2014) Policy Paper: *The politics of curriculum in schools*, Centre for Labour and Social Studies. Available at: http://classonline.org.uk/docs/2014_Policy_Paper_-_The_politics_of_curriculum_in_schools.pdf (Accessed: 31 October 2017).

Wyse, D., Baumfield, V., Egan, D. and Hayward, L. (2013) *Creating the curriculum*. Abingdon: Routledge.

6 Supporting core skills

Angela Sawyer, Andrew Sheehan and Ian Tinley

CHAPTER OVERVIEW AND AIMS

- To clarify the role of purpose and context for writing

- To consider the use of dialogic talk and oral rehearsal to develop reading comprehension

- To explore subject knowledge to highlight the importance of secure understanding in order to support children's progression and development in number

- To explain strategies for number acquisition and provide practical suggestions to exemplify key ideas and pre-empt errors and misconceptions

- To identify strategies to develop inquisitive individuals, searching for 'how' and 'why' scientific concepts work rather than the 'what' works

- To address, practically and creatively, how to engage children in thinking and working scientifically in order to promote a better understanding of the world around them

Introduction

This chapter will build on your understanding of the curriculum that began in Chapter 5. Here we explore in particular how English, mathematics and science are taught. Although this chapter is based on teaching the core subjects at primary level the content is appropriate for many of you who support pupils in secondary settings. Each subject will be discussed in turn, highlighting ways in which children gain knowledge, skills and understanding. The chapter will draw upon existing and current research which underpins teaching and learning and examines activities which promote investigative enquiry. Children learn best when they are motivated, enthused and engaged in activities which have a clear sense of purpose and interest; therefore the chapter will focus on creative teaching, both in and outside the classroom.

Throughout all three subjects we will identify the importance of speaking and listening to develop children's understanding and assess progress through paired, small group and whole class discussions. One key area identified will be the promotion of dialogic talk to support learning (Alexander, 2017).

The English curriculum

Once familiar with the progression of skills in current policy for the Early Years Foundation Stage (EYFS) and the National Curriculum, it is important to consider how these could be most effectively planned for in the classroom. Although there is a statutory programme of study which must be covered, this is just a starting point for learning, and there is no limit or restriction relating to the pedagogical approaches that can be used to deliver it.

The key areas in the programmes of study for teaching English are:

■ Speaking and listening – drama, group talk, performance, debate, discussion, using formal and informal language (including standard English)

■ Reading – early reading and phonics, decoding text, reading strategies, comprehension, reading for pleasure

■ Writing – transcription (handwriting, phonics and spelling), grammar and composition.

REFLECTION POINT

■ How confident are you in your understanding of the content and progression in subject knowledge and skills across the programmes of study for your chosen age ranges for English in each area?

Developing a context and purpose for teaching English

Within the current political and education climate, greater emphasis has been placed within the English curriculum on the importance of several key aspects, predominantly phonics, spelling and grammar. These are the areas that have been selected as indicators of progress through national testing in Key Stages 1 and 2 with the introduction of the phonics screening test in Year 1 and currently optional SATs testing in Year 2 along with statutory testing and assessment in Year 6 for reading, writing, spelling and grammar.

There is some concern amongst teachers, and professional writers such as Michael Morpurgo and Michael Rosen, that the English curriculum is being too restricted by testing, often with a narrow focus on spelling and grammar. If we do not develop children's imagination beyond this, they may produce 'technically' good writing, using a checklist of grammatical features to include, but could struggle to move beyond this to produce high-quality, engaging and original writing. Although teaching aspects of grammar can be beneficial, it needs to be taught in the context of how and why it impacts on the reader.

Consider the last book that you enjoyed. Although spelling and grammar may have played a key role in the way the language is structured, and therefore enhanced your reading experience, you may not have identified and analysed whether it had subordinate clauses, expanded noun phrases or two adjective sentences. Thus grammar and language is the tool that is used to support reading and writing rather than the master of it. Children should be encouraged to analyse the impact of the language and structures and consider the impact of the language being used in texts rather than simply being able to label language using technical terms.

> *Using grammar to help young writers to see through language, to see how language constructs socially-shaped meanings, to see how great language users break rules – this is where grammar realises its potential as a dynamic and vibrant element of English.*
>
> (Myhill, 2012: 22)

ACTIVITY

- Consider how changing the adjectives and adverbial phrases in these sentences impacts upon the reader's perception of the character and the event:

  The handsome, young mechanic raced through the lanes, like a rocket, in his imposing Cadillac Convertible.

  or

  The gnarled, wrinkled gentleman chugged down the lane, like a snail, in his dusty Cadillac Convertible.

Grammar should be identified for its effectiveness and impact on the reader and taught in the context of authentic reading and writing experiences rather than in isolation.

Children engage with and make better progress in English when they have a context for their learning (Cremin *et al.*, 2015), so as practitioners, we should be encouraging children's motivation and passion. In order to do this, writing should be incorporated into a task that is necessary and relevant to their lives (Vygotsky, 1978). We should aim to create a 'hook' to engage the children, using a range of creative and imaginative contexts, to write for a purpose and then identify opportunities to share that work with a wider audience so that the children can see that their work is valued.

CASE STUDY 6.1

The nature reserve

A class of Year 5 children were asked to debate the closure of a local nature reserve and consider what the land could be used for if it were to be closed.

Students visited the reserve and members of each group were asked to take photographs of either:

a) positive images which supported their discussion to keep the reserve open

b) negative images to provide evidence as to why the reserve should be closed and the land used for something else.

(continued)

(continued)

Whilst onsite at the nature reserve, the children filmed a television news report to upload onto the school website, inviting other pupils and parents to contribute their views in an online forum. The children then organised a debate, taking on the roles of different members of the community: council officials, children, residents whose homes back onto the reserve, dog walkers, the environmental agency and the housing association who wish to purchase the land. Each group had 10 minutes to present their case to the forum using their choice of any written medium to support them, for example, a presentation/leaflet/letter/poem.

REFLECTION POINTS

- What creative approaches to teaching English have you observed in your school?

- Are English lessons planned so that children write for a purpose and audience?

- How are children encouraged to share or publish their writing?

Using talk effectively to support learning

Although the progression of speaking and listening skills has been omitted in the current National Curriculum, it clearly identifies that talk can, and should, be used effectively to promote and develop children's thinking and to support learning in the classroom This can be achieved through planning opportunities for both formal and informal speaking and listening: role-play or improvised drama, debates, hot-seating, talk partners, presentations, performances and group discussions, such as the snowball or the jigsaw approach. It is important to allow children time to orally rehearse their ideas: if they cannot articulate their thoughts out loud then they are unlikely to be able to write them down.

In many classrooms, the use of talk partners is common practice to allow children an opportunity to share their thoughts and ideas with another person before sharing them with a larger group. Children, and adults, cannot always answer a question immediately after it has been asked and therefore need some time to consider what the question might mean and how it could be answered. To develop the effective use of talk partners further in lessons, each partner could be asked to focus on a different aspect of the learning so that both partners have something new or different to contribute to the discussion. For example, watching a short animated trailer to promote a new book for children, one partner might focus on the images, and the other on the words or music used in the advert, and then discuss in their pairs how each is used to persuade the reader.

Dialogic talk and group discussions

'Dialogic teaching harnesses the power of talk to engage children, stimulate and extend their thinking, and advance their learning and understanding' (Alexander, 2017: 4). In order to develop effective group discussions, Robin Alexander (2017) advocates the use of dialogic talk. Rather than group talk being teacher led, and sometimes dominated, he recommends that discussions should be:

- collective: teachers and children address learning tasks together, whether as a group or as a class

- reciprocal: teachers and children listen to each other in an equal partnership of mutual learning, sharing ideas and considering alternative viewpoints

- cumulative: teachers and children build on their own and each other's ideas and extend them into coherent lines of thinking and enquiry

- supportive: children articulate their ideas freely, without fear of embarrassment over 'wrong' answers; and they help each other to reach common understandings

- purposeful: teachers plan and steer classroom talk with specific educational goals in view.

The adult role, for example, in a whole class discussion would be to orchestrate or facilitate the talk, encouraging children to build on and refer back to previous answers, rather than to lead or dominate the questioning and discussion.

One example of this is 'Pose, Pause, Pounce, Bounce':

Pose and Pause – ask the question and pause for a response, allowing thinking time to answer.

Pounce – select a child using a random strategy method rather than hands-up, for example using lollipop sticks with the children's names on picked out of a cup. In random selection the expectation is that any child could be asked and therefore needs to be actively listening and following the discussion rather than waiting for someone else to put their hand up.

Bounce – bounce the first answer straight onto another student to respond using questions such as:

- Do you agree with . . . . . .'s comment? Why/why not?
- Can you explain a little further . . .?
- Why do you think that . . .?
- How could we explain . . .?

This would encourage the children to listen more actively to each other if a response is expected and hopefully ensure that certain children do not dominate discussions.

Questioning to develop comprehension

In relation to impact on pupil progress and outcomes, the use of open-ended, challenging questioning to promote comprehension and extend children's thinking is considered to be one of the most effective strategies. Research by Webster *et al.* (2016) into maximising the effect of adult support in the classroom identified, for example, that where the adult used higher-order questions, linked to Bloom's taxonomy (1956) to extend the pupils' thinking, the children made greater progress in their reading comprehension. When planning reading sessions, it is important to identify the focus and type of questioning that might be used in the session and consider examples of questions that could be asked to enable children to develop greater understanding of the text at all ages and levels of ability.

Table 6.1 Example of higher-order questions which could be used to develop reading comprehension

Higher-order question	Features	Example	Little Red Riding Hood
Applying	Children can: • apply information in different contexts • transfer knowledge from one context to another • make links with other stories	• Can you think of another story that has a similar theme..? • Which other stories have openings like this? • Which other author handles time in this way?	• Can you think of another story where the character is in danger? • Do you know of any other stories that are set in a forest?
Analysing	Children can: • build on existing knowledge • infer and deduce meanings • infer the author's intentions • analyse the text • express opinions and preferences	• What makes you think that . . .? • How do you feel about . . .? • Why do you think the author included . . . in the text ? • How has the author used . . .?	• Why do you think that Little Red Riding Hood went into the forest, even though she knew it was dangerous?

Synthesising	Children can: • take an idea and reapply it in a different context • restructure text • innovate text • take a critical stance • construct an argument/debate • predict	• What is your opinion and what evidence is there to support this? • What would this character do (in a different situation)? • How does the character's view affect the way that you think about . . .?	• What do you think about the wolf and the way he behaved? • Compare different versions of the same story – there are many versions from a wide range of countries and settings, for example, *Little Red Hot* by Eric Kimmel (2013), set in Texas.
Evaluating	Children can: • make judgements • compare and contrast • interrogate and evaluate the story • put forward evidence and reasoning	• What makes this a successful story? • Justify your opinion about . . . • Could it be better if . . .? • Is it better than . . . ?	• Which part of the story did you like best and why? • What would have made the story better?
Creating	Children can: • alter the original story • create their own story	• How would this story change if it was in a different time/setting? • Can you create a new story where a character tries to help someone but ends up in danger?	• Use the structure of Little Red Riding Hood to create a new story about a character who sets off on a journey but ends up in danger.

REFLECTION POINTS

Consider and evaluate the type of talk that you use in the classroom.

▦ How much time is spent on 'teacher' talk?

▦ What opportunities are there for promoting 'dialogic' talk in groups or as a whole class?

▦ How can you use questioning more effectively to develop children's thinking and comprehension?

Summary

Although the National Curriculum is the statutory guidance for what should be taught in school, it is best viewed as a starting point and the bare bones of what must be taught. The challenge for teachers and TAs is not only how to plan to ensure that all aspects of English are covered from the programme of study, but how to do it in a way that engages the children and promotes a lifelong passion for language and literacy. Ensuring that it is taught in an engaging and purposeful context is the key to ensuring that children's writing moves beyond a tick-list of features to include being 'creative' in its widest sense.

The maths curriculum

Introduction

In our experience of teaching mathematics to children, students and teachers, there seem to be three distinct groups of learning attitudes: excitement and engagement; fear and trepidation, or those who fall somewhere in between. You have probably already decided which category you fall into and this decision was probably based on how your teacher and test/exam results made you feel about mathematics, and this feeling remains with you today. You have already made the decision that you want to teach children, therefore as a professional, you will either want to pass on your love of mathematics or make sure the next generation of children form the love of mathematics which eluded you. In order to do this we need to consider how children learn to be successful in mathematics and how they can easily become confused and disengaged. This will be explored later in the chapter but before we do this, we need to consider how and why mathematics teaching has changed over recent years.

Introduction of national numeracy strategy

As we discussed in Chapter 3, the National Curriculum of 1988 gave schools a national syllabus for teaching mathematics from Key Stage 1 to Key Stage 4. Over the years this has been revised several times, with the latest version being published in 2013 (DfE, 2013).

In 1998 and on the back of the new government's landslide political victory in the previous year, under their manifesto promise of 'education, education, education' the government invested huge sums of money to target literacy and mathematics in primary schools before turning their attention to literacy and numeracy in secondary schools. In primary schools, mathematics support came in the form of numeracy subject knowledge training for serving teachers and 'guidance' documents known as the 'framework for teaching mathematics R–Y6' which set out mathematics expectations for different primary year groups. For example, by Year 2 children should be able to 'know their 2, 5 and 10 times tables'. This document gave teachers skill-based objectives (e.g. count on 1–9 within any two-digit number) which could be used to teach and assess pupil progress. The 'framework' also suggested a lesson structure, with lessons starting with mental maths practice (e.g. all children chanting tables, naming shapes, counting in multiples etc.) before the teacher moved on to teach the 'main part of the lesson' using objectives from the framework. The lesson concluded with a lesson review, known as the 'plenary'. The framework also suggested how long a lesson should last, so mathematics lessons were therefore known as the 'numeracy hour'. The national numeracy strategy and national literacy strategy 'frameworks' merged in 2006 to become the Primary National Strategy which amalgamated and simplified both frameworks to become one primary framework for literacy and numeracy. In 2009, the Coalition government disbanded the primary national strategy so, for the first time in many years, schools returned to teach the National Curriculum in ways they decided.

A recent development in primary mathematics is the introduction of 'schemes' such as 'Maths Makes Sense' or 'Singapore Mathematics'. Schemes range from prescriptive lesson plans to suggested activities. Schemes tend to polarise teacher opinion: those who believe mathematics can be broken down and taught using prescribed plans and those who believe teaching mathematics relies on secure subject knowledge and creative ways to engage children with a broad, varied, interesting mathematics curriculum.

Influences of testing on the mathematics curriculum

In order to consider one other influence on the mathematics curriculum I would like you to think of a course or module that you have studied recently which required you to undertake an assessment: perhaps a written exam assignment or test in which you will be graded. No doubt you wanted to do your best to ensure your grade reflected your hard work and commitment. I am sure you found out early on what you needed to do to pass/obtain the best grade possible. This may have caused you to prioritise your efforts toward the assessment perhaps even at the expense of other aspects of the course. Your tutor may have even done the same by encouraging you to look at past exam papers or explain what you need to do to pass. The point I am trying to make is that assessments can influence what and how the subject matter is taught and the learner can get caught up in exam practice at the expense of depth of learning. One other important point to consider is all the potential worry and stress that may result and the fear of what might happen if you are not successful. Children are no different. Since their phased introduction in 1991, primary school children have been involved with national testing for pupils aged 7 and 11. All subsequent governments have continued to test pupils despite a wealth of evidence from professionals that they do not improve teaching and learning. A frequent response from student teachers on teaching placement is that many children are engaged in SATs practice in Year 6 from Easter. SATs are therefore likely to affect what is taught in the classroom and also have the potential to affect children's perceptions and create anxieties about mathematics.

REFLECTION POINTS

Think about the last time you were tested for mathematics.

- How did you feel?

- How did the test influence your learning of mathematics?

- Think back to the last time you visited a primary mathematics lesson. How similar or different was the lesson to the structure of the 'numeracy hour'?

How do children learn mathematics?

You came across the term 'learning theory' in Chapter 4. We should really refer to 'learning theories' as many academics have researched and written at length about how children learn mathematics. There is common agreement that children learn in complex ways and they are influenced by many factors. As teachers, we need to have an understanding of factors which we can control so we can give children the very best opportunities to learn. You may have heard the term 'behaviour theory'. This is a broad term used to explain that learning takes place when the respondent (in this context a child in your class) responds to stimulus and 'learns' from the experience. In the context of mathematics, perhaps the most obvious example would be a child learning their tables by rote, then reciting a given multiplication fact instantly when asked. In this case the stimulus is the question and the answer is the response or 'behaviour'.

There is another group of academics known as constructivists, who believe learning takes place when the learner is placed in a state of 'equilibrium' (state of mind beyond knowing): learning takes place by the learner constructing a mental pathway to re-gain equilibrium. An example of this could be a learner knowing their 5 times tables but not knowing how to work out 5 x 35. Once the child learns that 35 is made up of 30 and 5 and that 30 is made up of 3 tens they can use this knowledge, combined with their pre-existing knowledge of the 5 times table to firstly work out 5 x 30, then 5 x 5 before adding both answers together. Some children may realise how to do this on their own, but social constructivists believe children learn with support – usually someone showing or explaining things to them. The term used for this is 'scaffolding'. It is vital, therefore, that teachers have good mathematical subject knowledge and know how to explain mathematical skills and knowledge accurately.

We must also consider social influences on how children learn mathematics. How children are made to feel about their progress and achievement in mathematics cannot be overstated. Children need to be praised when they have a go and try – even if they get the wrong answer; but more importantly they need to be corrected and shown how to get the right answer in a manner which leaves them feeling positive and ready to have another try next time. Children will soon learn not to try if they are made to feel embarrassed or uneasy.

Modelling

Many children and adults find many aspects of mathematics extremely abstract so we must make sure children 'see' how mathematics works by modelling. Many children struggle with place value, which is a term used to describe how our number system works. Basically, our number system is based on powers of 10. For instance, the number 123 is made up of 3 units (or 'ones') 2 tens and 1 hundred. As we move from right to left the value of each number column increases by a power of 10. Similarly, as the columns move to the right, the value of the number column decreases by a power of 10. This system can be extended to decimals, so 3.45 is made up of 3 units, 4 tenths and 5 hundredths. In order to show how the number system works, place value materials can be used to model the number system. These are readily available in most schools.

Another way to show how whole numbers beyond nine are formed is by using 'arrow cards'. By matching the pointed part of the cards together, children will see how the number 123 is partitioned into 100 plus 20 plus 3. There are many difficult 'big ideas' in mathematics so it is vital that teachers model concepts using a range of resources and allow children to experience the resources themselves.

Addressing misconceptions

As teachers we have absolute responsibility to teach children precisely and use methods which are accurate. In order to consider this, as a good mathematician you probably have tried and tested ways of working out calculations quickly and accurately. For instance if you know $5 \times 6 = 30$ you can easily work out that $5 \times 600 = 3000$ and you probably use your knowledge of $5 \times 6 = 30$ to realise that 5×600 requires little thought beyond adding two zeros to 30 to arrive at your answer of $5 \times 6 = 3000$. However, this method may confuse children because it does not explain how the answer is formed. Adding 2 zeros when multiplying by 100 is not helpful to children when they are learning to multiply, because it is in conflict with how the number system works. A much clearer explanation is to calculate 5×600 by firstly factorising 600 into 6×100 then calculate $5 \times 6 \times 100$. One further difficulty arises when children start to multiply using decimal numbers because 1.5×10 does not equal 1.50! It is generally accepted that when children have poor interconnections within mathematics ideas they are more likely to make mistakes (Hansen, 2017: 2); therefore it is important that teachers should avoid the use of 'quick fix rules' in mathematics as these lead to misunderstanding and misconceptions.

CASE STUDY 6.2

Planning a party

Children in a Year 4 class are planning an end-of-year party. The children decide what to buy so the teacher delegates purchasing to Red group and Blue group who have been taught to multiply by multiples of 10. The children plan the party for 30 children so the teacher is confident the children should find the task relatively easy. The teacher has taught the children to multiply by 30 using 'times by 3 then times by 10'. The teacher has also taught 'money' so the children are able to convert pounds to pence and visa-versa. This is a copy of the children's planning notes:

Blue Group

	Cost of 1 unit	Cost of 10 units	Cost of 30 items
packet of crisps	25p	250p or £2.50	£7.50
bottle of drink	90p	900p or £9.00	£27.00
bag of sweets	£1.25	£12.50	£37.50
sandwich	£1.50	£15.00	£45.00

Red Group

	Cost of 1 unit	Cost of 10 units	Cost of 30 items
packet of crisps	25p	250p or £2.50	£7.50
bottle of drink	90p	900p or £9.00	£27.00
bag of sweets	£1.25	£1.250	£3.750
sandwich	£1.50	£1.500	£4.500

Blue Group's work suggests the children are able to multiply whole and decimal numbers by 10 accurately and use this information to calculate the cost of 30 items.

Red Group children arrive at the correct answer for 10 packets of crisps and 10 bottles of drink but arrive at incorrect answers for the bags of sweets and sandwiches. This could be because their method for multiplying by 10 is to 'add a zero' to £1.25 and £1.50 – to arrive at £1.250 and £1.50. These errors may have been used to calculate 30 items.

Summary

It is very easy to fall into the trap that in order to be a good teacher of mathematics, one needs to be good at mathematics and know the content of the National Curriculum for the year group being taught. Whilst both of these are important, we hope this chapter has given you an insight how this is a limited and simplistic view of teaching mathematics. Mathematics is much more than this: it is about providing children with real-life problems and encouraging them to find real-life solutions; modelling mathematics accurately (Worthington and Carruthers 2006: 191); addressing children's misconceptions (Hansen 2017: 1) and showing children 'connections' (Haylock and Cockburn, 2017: 10) within mathematics as well as many other factors which I hope this chapter has inspired you to find out by further reading.

The science curriculum

Introduction

Some of you may think back to your own science lessons and remember memorising facts from a textbook about the periodic table or how forces work. But science is so much more than the knowledge that makes its way into school books. Science is about the process of exploration and discovery, learning something new about the natural world, and how such new discoveries have changed the face of science and technology today.

Science itself generates awe and wonder and it is important to instil and encourage children to find science lessons an exciting and intriguing part of the school day. You may have found science difficult at some point in your learning but don't be despondent. Even the greatest scientific minds would have been challenged at some point in their career. Of course science involves learning facts relating to biology, chemistry and physics but it also encompasses creative problem-solving, communicating with others and logical reasoning, to name a few skills. Science incorporates a broad set of activities. Teachers in primary schools often find themselves teaching science topics that are unfamiliar and find it difficult to teach at the limit of their own subject knowledge. When we find ourselves faced with such topics it is important to read more than we need to know, because if we are developing enquiring minds there will be children asking questions beyond the scope of the lesson.

Science in the National Curriculum

The science National Curriculum (DfE, 2013) has three clear aims: to develop children's science knowledge and conceptual understanding, to develop their understanding of the nature and processes of science and to understand the uses and implications of science in everyday life. The new science curriculum, introduced in 2013, has greater challenge associated with scientific terminology where 'working scientifically' is woven through all aspects of pedagogical content knowledge; it is the way by which children will engage and learn science and is suggested to be at the heart of every good science lesson. Interestingly there is much more focus on outdoor learning and engagement, in a sustained way through the progressive year groups. The National Curriculum also includes a breakdown of statutory and non-statutory requirements for each year group across Key Stage 1, Lower Key Stage 2 and Upper Key Stage 2. In the Early Years, children need to focus on the world around them and how things link together, working through the goals of scientific exploration. For Key Stages 3 and 4 'working scientifically', the subject content areas Biology, Chemistry and Physics are structured strands.

REFLECTION POINTS

- Discuss what you think children know about science before they start school, or before they begin secondary school. How will this make an impact on their learning?

- Why it is important to know what a child is really thinking?

When we consider the start of a science lesson, staff may focus on getting the children to write down the learning objective or lesson title. This can lead to missed opportunities to grab the children's attention. Instead, begin with the science phenomenon, create awe and wonder simultaneously within a context that makes sense to the children and has purpose. It is also important that we elicit children's ideas about their science knowledge or concepts during the start of a topic or lesson so that we can address any issues that may arise. Remember children are not passive recipients of knowledge but that conceptual development involves the active construction of new knowledge (Harlen, 2013: 12), a process that produces a change in ideas. The scientific view frequently makes use of ideas based on things that are not observable by the children, such as water vapour, unseen forces and vibrations in the air. In making sense of such ideas in science, the child is involved in a process requiring constant refinement, redefinition and interpretation.

We must consider that numerous children will continue to build knowledge from their current understandings. Such ideas are often intuitive and fruitful to them and hence children can often be resistant to change. However harmless you believe this to be, possessing misunderstandings where children have not understood the scientific idea can have serious implications on an individual's learning and progression, not only through the topic but throughout future key stages. Only when we ask the questions do we truly find out what a child believes and hence establish a more accurate starting point. Often science requires children to link together several unseen abstract concepts; therefore complex understanding needs to be built up slowly, layer upon layer.

There are numerous teaching strategies you could use to help discover what a child is truly thinking. Such methods include: card sorting activities, getting pupils to represent their ideas visually in drawings or diagrams, linking ideas and scientific terminology by completing concept maps on a particular topic, using concept cartoons to pre-empt children's possible ideas and getting them to discuss which character they believe is correct about a scientific concept and why, using toys and puppets to stimulate dialogic talk, exploring ideas or questions using scientific apparatus and most simple of all listening to children talking in groups. Any of the methods suggested above will engage hands and minds into 'thinking and doing'. Most importantly, the children should have a vehicle to summarise and express their ideas and understanding clearly and without fear of getting something wrong.

Teaching strategies

The primary science curriculum has changed since 2013 from being concerned with a child's achievement through levels, to focus on 'mastery' of a subject area or topic. Hence there needs to be a level of challenge within the planning process to engage the children to think about the question in a different way and how such knowledge or scientific concept is a spoke in the wheel of the 'big idea'. In this context, never before has pedagogical content knowledge and teaching strategies been as pivotal in helping children to understand scientific concepts.

Below is a list of possible strategies, methods and suggestions which could help children understand tricky subject matter:

■ Use models, analogues or illustrations to support the explanation.

■ Use a physical demonstration, picture or artefacts to base discussions around.

■ Simplify the science concept so that communication is at the pupil's age-appropriate level.

■ Break down the science ideas into smaller easily understood parts.

■ Backtrack and simplify an idea if the pupil clearly does not understand the first explanation.

■ Relate the science idea to an event that is familiar to the pupil.

■ With younger children, weave the question or explanation into a fictitious story if this seems to help.

Adapted from Sharp *et al.* (2014: 59)

REFLECTION POINTS

■ What kinds of learning activities or teaching strategies have you seen or used to develop or assess a child's scientific understanding?

■ How could you use these methods to address a specific subject matter? Examples include habitats, plant growth, forces, electricity, earth and space.

Working scientifically

You will find many descriptions of scientific enquiry or 'working scientifically'. Most discuss the skills children need to develop so that they can collect and use evidence to describe models and theories. This in turn helps them to understand how the natural and made world works. A key aim of science education is for you to develop the scientific skills of the children you are working with, in areas such as observing, collecting evidence or data, making predictions, testing possible explanations and interpreting and evaluating findings.

The majority of children enjoy practical work as an alternative to other teaching approaches and as an approach to autonomous working. Furthermore, it can provide cognitive advantages in helping children to learn science, especially when an explicit strategy is used to link ideas and activities together. When completing practical investigations it is important to encourage the child or group of children to: share their ideas and construct understanding together, propose possible explanations of observations and use them to make predictions that can be questioned or tested, record results in suitable ways using appropriate scientific vocabulary, address and attempt to explain results by communicating what they have done verbally in a drawing, table or graph and reflect self-critically on the process (adapted from the ASE Guide to Primary Science (Harlen, 2013: 7).

Working scientifically does not simply apply to practical work, though of course that is a significant part of it. Children need to be encouraged to carry out investigations where the aim is to allow them to use and to develop concepts, skills and procedural understanding. They should have some responsibility for deciding what to do and how to do it; putting it simply, be allowed to think for themselves. If children are encouraged to make choices, then they can use their knowledge and skills to extend their understanding and make progress even when things go wrong. Remember that children's scientific questions should be answered using a range of different scientific enquiries which include: grouping and classifying, pattern seeking, fair testing, observing over time and researching secondary sources.

Fair testing is only one of the strands of working scientifically but is usually the type of enquiry most teachers and children alike are familiar with. It is of paramount importance for breadth and depth of understanding that pupils are immersed in all five types of enquiry mentioned above, each as important as the other, as without such enquiry skills the pupil will not be exposed to the broad range of skills required to successfully understand concepts and theories in science. However, for your own development the section of the chapter discussing 'fair testing' is specifically addressed because it is the most widely implemented by teachers when developing enquiry skills.

CASE STUDY 6.3

Thinking scientifically

A Year 5 teacher encouraged children to 'think scientifically and problem solve' during a stand-alone science lesson. She asked the children to work in small groups to create a sand clock that always lasted 2 minutes. The children were given a selection of resources which they had to choose from, that included plastic and polythene cups and a range of different grain sands. The children were encouraged to discuss what variables they had to take into account and plan a fair test. Within the discussions the children addressed numerous high-order thinking aspects and by working together

(continued)

(continued)

thought of many different strategies. Eventually most of the groups decided to change the size of the hole the sand would flow through, made within the base of one of the plastic cups. They then had to alter the amount of sand within the cup as necessary until they could confidently time 2 minutes exactly. The whole class enjoyed the investigation thoroughly. There was plenty of dialogic talk between groups of pupils and between staff and pupils. Importantly a myriad of investigative skills were involved to solve the problem.

How will you record the data/results?

Fair testing

In order to carry out an investigation a student must first understand the concept of fair testing. In lower Key Stage 2, students are beginning to understand that for investigations to be fair you must only change one thing or variable for your findings to be valid. For example, when investigating what would be the best parachute for a skydiver, factors you could investigate include the size of the parachute, the shape of the parachute and the material the parachute is made from; however, only one variable would be changed and all other factors or variables must be kept the same or constant. This allows the findings to be valid and where applicable a pattern in results could be interpreted.

A few key questions direct the children's attention to points they should think about before starting the 'fair test' such as:

■ What are we trying to find out?

■ What are we going to change?

■ What are we keeping the same?

■ What are we going to measure?

■ What equipment will we need?

■ What do you predict will happen?

Adapted from Sharp *et al.* (2014: 18)

To help plan and structure an investigation there are numerous writing frames available on the market which may aid children to access learning. However, a word of warning: we should take care that such writing frames do not become straitjackets and take attention from the investigation itself.

Ways to support a group of children during a science lesson

There are numerous teaching strategies you could employ to engage a child or group of children you are working with during a science lesson. Provide them with numerous hands-on practical activities (each member of the group should be involved) to help embed the concept, making sure they predict what they think will happen. However, you need to bear in mind that a number of primary schools will have limited science resources. Therefore, to address the possible problem of limited practical equipment, when not all members of the group can be involved practically, try to encourage other members of the group to ask questions and discuss what is happening and why. Challenge the group's ideas by constantly asking open-ended questions and getting them to respond in full sentences with explanations, rather than giving one word responses. Importantly, encourage them to think and make links between different science concepts and topics that they have previously encountered. But remember there is not a 'one size fits all' approach. Be flexible and use your experience and intuition; if a technique is not working, stop and try another.

Summary

Science encompasses many aspects of the natural world and it is impossible to address every avenue with great detail. Therefore our role is to engage and motivate students to appreciate the range of abstract and conceptual concepts that drive science forward as well as the daily encounters every student will have. Each section of the chapter is underpinned by ways to develop learners into inquisitive individuals searching for 'how' and 'why' scientific concepts work, rather than the 'what' works. Although fair testing is addressed in more depth, other strands of working scientifically are discussed and signposted as being just as important to a student's development and understanding of science. Importantly the chapter introduces practical and creative ways on how we can engage children in thinking and working scientifically so they can better understand the world around them.

Chapter summary

In this chapter we have explored how English, mathematics and science may be taught, drawing upon examples from current research, highlighting the ways in which children gain knowledge, skills and understanding. We have identified how speaking and listening, and in particular dialogic talk, can support children's understanding. We have considered how children learn best when they are motivated, enthused and engaged in activities which have a clear sense of purpose and interest both in and outside the classroom. Each subject has provided practical suggestions to exemplify key ideas, including investigative enquiry, and considered how to pre-empt and address misconceptions.

FURTHER READING

Alexander, R. (2017) *Towards dialogic teaching: rethinking classroom talk* (5th edn). Thirsk: Dialogos UK Limited.

Cremin, T., Reedy, D., Bearne, E. and Dombey, H. (2015) *Teaching English creatively*. London: Routledge.

Haylock, D. and Manning, R. (2014) *Mathematics explained for primary teachers*. London: Sage.

Peacock, G., Sharp, J., Johnsey, R. and Wright D. (2014) *Primary science knowledge and understanding* (7th edn). Exeter: Learning Matters.

Sharp, J., Peacock, G., Johnsey, R., Simon, S., Smith, R., Cross, A. and Harris, D. (2014) *Primary science teaching theory and practice* (7th edn). Exeter: Learning Matters.

Skemp, R. (1971) *The psychology of learning mathematics*. Middlesex: Penguin.

References

Alexander, R. (2017) *Towards dialogic teaching: rethinking classroom talk* (5th edn). Thirsk: Dialogos UK Limited.

Bloom, B.S. (ed.) (1956) *Taxonomy of educational objectives, handbook I: the cognitive domain*. New York: David McKay Co, Inc.

Cooke, V. and Howard, C. (2014) *Practical ideas for teaching primary science*. Northwich: Critical Publishing.

Cremin, T., Reedy, D., Bearne, E. and Dombey, H. (2015) *Teaching English creatively*. London: Routledge.

Department for Education (DfE) (2013) *The national curriculum in England: framework document*. London: DfE.

Department for Education (DfE) (2017) *Statutory framework for the early years foundation stage: setting the standards for learning, development and care for children from birth to five*. London: DfE.

Dunne, M. and Peacock, A. (2015) *Primary science: a guide to teaching practice* (2nd edn). London: Sage.

Hansen, A. (2017) *Children's errors in mathematics* (4th edn). London: Sage.

Harlen, W. (ed.) (2013) *ASE guide to primary science education*. Hatfield: ASE.

Haylock, D. and Cockburn, A. (2017) *Understanding mathematics for young children: a guide for teaching children 3–7* (5th edn). London: Sage.

Myhill, D. (2012) 'The role for grammar in the curriculum', in *Meeting high expectations: looking for the heart of English*. Available from: http://heartofenglish.com (Accessed: 1 October 2012).

Peacock, G., Sharp, J., Johnsey, R. and Wright, D. (2014) *Primary science knowledge and understanding* (7th edn). Exeter: Learning Matters.

Sharp, J., Peacock, G., Johnsey, R., Simon, S., Smith, R., Cross, A. and Harris, D. (2014) *Primary science teaching theory and practice* (7th edn). Exeter: Learning Matters.

STEM Learning (2017) *SPACE (science processes and concepts exploration) research reports (1990–98)*. Available at: https://stem.org.uk/resources/collection/3324/space-research-reports (Accessed: 10 November 2017).

Vygotsky, L.S. (1978) *Mind in society*. Cambridge, MA: Harvard University Press.

Webster, R., Russell, A. and Blatchford, P. (2016) *Maximising the impact of teaching assistants: guidance for school leaders and teachers*. London: Routledge.

Worthington, M. and Carruthers, E. (2006) *Children's mathematics: making marks, making meaning* (2nd edn). London: Sage.

7

Children and technology

Stephen Dixon

CHAPTER OVERVIEW AND AIMS

■ To explore the use of technology in schools

■ To consider ways in which teaching assistants support learning and teaching with technology

■ To explore the impact of web 2.0 tools and apps

■ To understand online safety and ethical issues surrounding the use of technology

■ To consider different types of assistive technology and their role in promoting inclusive practice

---

Introduction

This chapter will introduce you to a range of ideas exploring the use of technology in schools, with a focus on its impact on the learning and teaching process and the role of the TA in supporting this, whether in the classroom or dedicated information technology (IT) labs. Whilst recent curriculum changes are touched upon, such as the shift from information and communication technology (ICT) to computer science, the chapter will focus on three major strands: **online safety issues**, particularly in relation to ethical concerns, online behaviour and safeguarding; the **rise of new technologies and digital media,** with attention paid to the rise of web 2.0 tools and apps and their potential for learning; and **overcoming barriers to using ICT**, with special emphasis being placed on the role of assistive technologies in the classroom. Throughout the chapter, you will be encouraged to reflect on your own technological skills and training needs. A range of examples will be used throughout the discussion, as well as useful resources identified to support you in your practice.

Context – the use of technology in schools

It is always difficult to discuss the use of technology in education, in that any exploration of specific technologies, tools or apps can quickly become out of date. As such, and although examples of use of technology will be touched upon, the main focus of this chapter is the issue raised by the use of learning technologies, rather than the tools themselves. Although there are significant differences between schools in the ways in which technology is configured and used, its use is now so ubiquitous as to be unremarkable. Schools now have access to a wide range of technological devices and tools (many of which can be incorporated into one device), so the new TA in particular may be met with a bewildering array of hardware and software that is used to support learning and teaching, from standard laptops and PCs to interactive whiteboards, tablets and hand-held devices (which themselves may hold a wide range of learning apps), MP3 recorders and players, video-recording equipment, and programmable turtles and robots, for example. Similarly, the majority of schools, both primary and secondary, now use a virtual learning environment (VLE) to support learning and teaching (Ofsted, 2011).

Despite recent curriculum changes, the use of technology in schools can be seen as unique in that it is both a discrete subject in itself, as well as being used to support other subjects throughout the curriculum, such as in embedding the use of interactive whiteboards in all aspects of daily teaching and learning. The majority of schools now use technology in order to equip pupils with the skills necessary to become independent learners and, as such, you may find that technology-enhanced teaching sessions are much more interactive in nature and practical in focus. Pupils may often be given group or individual tasks to use learning technologies in support of their learning in other subjects, such as in the use of internet sites to support research for a science topic or taking digital photographs for a history display.

The use of technology can be seen as both transformative and as an important life skill, in that its successful use not only equips children with the necessary skills to participate in their continuing education, but also for their future lives in the workplace. Children need to locate, explore, analyse, exchange and present information, as well as developing the necessary skills to use information in a discriminating and effective way. This is particularly important in terms of pupils developing their language and communication skills, and enabling them to manipulate information both creatively and appropriately. As the Department for Education (DfE) highlights, a high-quality computing education equips pupils to use computational thinking and creativity to understand and change the world. Computing has deep links with mathematics, science and design and technology, and provides insights into both natural and artificial systems (DfE, 2013).

As a TA, you will thus need to support a child's learning not just through the application of technology, by applying hardware and software to monitor and control events, for example, but also in allowing pupils to explore issues of technology, such as their attitudes towards it, its role in society, and how they can apply their skills and knowledge to their learning in other areas. Such issues are particularly pertinent to concepts of digital literacy and online safety, where children will need to learn about issues of accuracy, security and confidentiality, as well as about how to make informed, safe and sensible decisions when using technology – these are explored in greater detail below.

The recognition of the need to improve children's digital literacy can be seen by its attempted address in the new Primary Curriculum of September 2014, where there is a much greater emphasis on the teaching of computer science and programming. This shift from ICT to computing aims to ensure that all pupils:

- can understand and apply the fundamental principles and concepts of computer science, including abstraction, logic, algorithms and data representation

- can analyse problems in computational terms, and have repeated practical experience of writing computer programs in order to solve such problems

- can evaluate and apply information technology, including new or unfamiliar technologies, analytically to solve problems, and

- are responsible, competent, confident and creative users of information and communication technology.

(DfE, 2013)

You may find, however, that many fellow staff still discuss the use of technology in terms of ICT rather than computing (indeed, your school will almost definitely still have a senior member of staff acting as an ICT co-ordinator). Whilst there is a greater emphasis on aspects of computer science in the new curriculum, as well as a stronger focus on specific computing knowledge, many suggest that the arguments over differences in terms between ICT and computing are redundant, as the latter still covers the broad application of technology that teachers are expected to use to enhance teaching and learning as appropriate (Turvey *et al.*, 2014).

Technology and the role of the TA

Within the educational setting, the TA has to perform a broad range of duties. Yet whereas much of a TA's workload may be taken up by working with pupils in very small groups or on a one-to-one basis, such as focussing on improving specific skills for short periods, this may change when you are supporting a technology-enhanced lesson or a computer science session. Most job descriptions for TA posts now include specific reference to the importance of the role in supporting the use of technology with pupils, such as supervising and supporting pupils ensuring their safety and access to learning; or being competent in the use of ICT and using ICT as a tool for teaching and learning. Expected duties may range from supporting pupils in using basic ICT as directed, to supporting the use of ICT in learning activities and developing pupils' competence and independence in its use.

TAs may be expected to make effective use of ICT to support learning or even have the ability to advise on appropriate deployment and use of specialist aid/resources/equipment. Indeed, many schools now employ dedicated technical teaching assistants, whose roles specifically relate to the provision of support in technology, such as in assisting in lessons in the ICT suite, supporting teachers in the use of learning technologies in other curriculum areas, routine maintenance and repair of hardware (including dealing with technical queries), and even running school computer clubs.

If the use of technology is seen as most effective where it is embedded across the curriculum, and not seen as separate from learning and teaching, then the role of the TA will obviously vary in supporting pupils to apply their knowledge of computing in their use of ICT in other subjects (DfE, 2013). Such duties may vary from the practical and mundane (although these are still important), such as checking that computer facilities work and that pupils can log in easily, and ensuring that programs such as internet browsers and Microsoft packages are working correctly. You may be expected to use technology in preparation for lessons, such as producing worksheets that pupils can use in either hard copy or online, or vetting the suitability of websites to be used in class or for pupils' research.

It is important to realise that you may also be the first port of call in ensuring that computer hardware is working correctly, such as checking that the keyboard and mouse work, or that the computer is linked correctly with the printer so that pupils can print off the work they have produced. If there are problems that you are unable to fix yourself, you will certainly be expected to liaise with the school's IT/technical support to solve these – part of your role in supporting the teacher and pupils is to ensure that technical issues are not eating into important learning time.

It is essential, then, that you feel comfortable with institutional procedures and systems. If you are not already familiar with your school's ICT policy, for example, you should ask to see a copy – this will give you an understanding of the school's aims and objectives for teaching and learning with technology. As well as outlining the roles and responsibilities of the school's staff, this will explain how the use of technology is monitored and recorded (as well as assessed), and may also outline various resources and schemes of work used in learning and teaching.

It is important, in your role as TA, that you reflect on your own IT skills and training needs. Technology is an area of the curriculum in which many TAs (and teaching staff) feel less comfortable – as Morris (2012: 7) highlights, 'TA skill levels were also generally reported to vary, with some TAs being labelled "experts" and others "technophobic dinosaurs" '. It is not uncommon for those TAs who feel least comfortable with technology to unconsciously use avoidance techniques. Other common barriers include lack of confidence, lack of skills, lack of support and lack of time, each of which can be overcome with the appropriate resources and mindset. When you begin in your role, you may find that you need basic training in more frequently used software, such as the school's VLE, for example. Obviously technology develops at a rapid rate and you will find that your school provides training and continuing professional development (CPD) sessions as new tools and software are integrated into the curriculum – some of these are explored below.

REFLECTION POINTS

Most schools now require some level of technological capability for all TA staff. You will, however, be expected to update and develop these skills as part of your ongoing CPD. For those new in post, the following questions may be useful:

- What skills do I have?
- Which particular skills do I need to develop?
- What software and hardware will I need to use?
- How will I be expected to use these to support learning and teaching?
- Have I read and understood the school's ICT policy?
- Do I know where to go to (including IT support staff) if I need help?

The impact of web 2.0 tools

It is difficult now to think of a world without mobile phones, digital television, MP3 players, touch-screen devices and wifi internet access – but remember that the children in your class will have no knowledge of a world without these things. Since 2005, and coupled with rise in bandwidth and broadband technology, there has been a marked rise in the number of user-friendly, interactive applications on the web, where even people with little technical skill can create and share content. This supposed second generation of web tools, or web 2.0, includes those sites used for video sharing, social bookmarking, instant messaging, social recommendation and discovery and file sharing, for example, as well as social networking sites, wikis, and online communication tools that emphasise both sharing and online collaboration.

Much has been written on how both web 2.0 tools and many modern educational apps can be empowering to learners; can be engaging and motivating in the classroom; and allow for sociable and collaborative creativity in learning – a large number of primary schools, for example, are now encouraging pupils to edit films and maintain blogs. Such tools are seen as increasing the emphasis on the 'C' of ICT, as one of the key features of web 2.0 is that of communication (Davies and Merchant, 2009). Many children and young people are already using a wide range of web 2.0 tools, be these smartphone or tablet apps, or communicating via MSN or Skype, notwithstanding the seemingly ubiquitous use of social networking sites such as Facebook. Importantly, the use of such tools has the potential to make learning fun, as well as allowing for collaboration and the development of important skills for the future.

It is important to remember, however, that all classes have children with widely differing digital abilities and to alleviate this, schools may group children by ability and set differentiated tasks. It is here that the role of the TA is crucial in supporting these individuals or groups. For more able pupils, this can often be problematic, as the Office for Standards in Education, Children's Services and Schools (Ofsted) has highlighted, 'Sometimes pupils' ICT capability was so good that it outstripped their teachers' subject knowledge and, as a result, their good progress was not sustained. In such circumstances, higher-attaining pupils often underachieved' (Ofsted, 2009: 9).

It is dangerous to assume, however, that you are supporting the learning and teaching of an entire generation of tech-savvy pupils. For example, research shows a strong correlation between technological competence and economic background, with children from poorer families often having lower levels of digital literacy. Even for pupils with access to a range of technological devices at home, the mismatch between their domestic use and that experienced in schools – what Selwyn (2006) calls the digital disconnect – particularly where the latter may be perceived as less advanced, can lead to issues of demotivation.

Further problematic is the common practice of schools blocking access to certain sites and services on grounds of online safety or bandwidth capability. It is not unusual, for example, for schools to even block access to commonly used video-sharing sites such as YouTube, despite their obvious educational potential and teacher and pupil enthusiasm for their use in lessons. This is also despite enjoinders from both researchers and even Ofsted that such approaches can be counter-productive in terms of e-safety: a child whose use of the internet is closely monitored at school will not necessarily develop the level of understanding required to use new technologies responsibly in other contexts (Ofsted, 2010).

Clearly, you will need to become familiar with your particular school's policy on the use of a range of web 2.0 tools and sites. In secondary schools, you may even find that some sites are available to certain year groups, but not others. More recently, schools have explored the use of web 2.0 tools to facilitate flipped learning, where delivery of lesson content takes place in the home and lesson-time is used for support and discussion, and here your role as a TA is crucial. Such approaches emphasise the collaborative and interactive nature of learning with web 2.0 – as Goodison (2002: 86) highlights, 'The transfer of learning in ICT is two-way: from home to school and from school to home, and just as siblings (and parents) play an important role at home, so do classmates at school'.

CASE STUDY 7.1

Kate and Marie

Kate is a KS2 teacher and ICT Co-ordinator in a primary school. With the support of Marie, her TA, she uses Aurasma, a freely available app, to enrich learning and motivate pupils in their Year 5 topic on the Ancient Egyptians. Aurasma is an augmented reality platform, using advanced image and pattern recognition to blend the real world with rich interactive content such as videos and animations called auras. With the help of the pupils, Kate and Marie have developed a display in their classroom, with pictures of pyramids, the Sphinx and the River Nile, as well as information on Ancient Egyptian clothing and jewellery, for example. In Aurasma, Kate and Marie have taken a picture of the display, and added auras to specific points in the picture. When a pupil points their tablet or hand-held device at the display, they can now not only see the original real-world image, but interact with the auras for further information and multimedia, such as a short film about the River Nile, an animation of mummification, and links to Ancient Egyptian artefacts and educational resources in the British Museum.

Online safety

When you read your school's ICT policy, you will quickly become aware of a range of tools that schools use to make their ICT systems secure. These are not just in place to support teaching and learning, for online safety affects every member of the school community. In your own professional practice, for example, you will also be expected to observe simple, everyday security measures such as logging out of secure systems, backing up data, not leaving computers unattended and not sharing password information. The safe and secure use of technology has an impact on a range of areas of statutory responsibility for schools, including safeguarding, health and safety, and data protection. If your role includes the recording of data on pupils, or even downloading resources, you will need to be aware of how such legislation affects this.

Ofsted (2011) has long recommended that schools continue to make e-safety a priority in the curriculum and as such, teaching staff (including TAs) need to understand the implications of using technology in school and, as part of their professional practice, provide suitable safeguards for pupils, including teaching them safe and responsible behaviour. Schools that address this most effectively will have a clear strategy for ICT that considers both safety and security issues. Part of your role may include ensuring that e-safety rules are displayed prominently for pupils to see, and ensuring that these are understood.

On a more practical level, there are a number of measures which schools adopt to address online safety issues. These may include the use of firewalls to prevent unauthorised access to networks and sensitive data, or simple encryption systems to maintain security or prevent hacking, particularly if a school has wifi technology. Whilst your school will almost definitely have anti-virus software, you may find that there are strict policies on staff using personal devices (laptops, phones, portable storage devices, etc) in order to strengthen this approach. Many schools also use simple software filters to restrict access to inappropriate online content, or block access to certain sites and services, despite the problems this may cause (see above). Schools will also regularly monitor the use of technology, particularly by keeping track of all accessed or downloaded internet material to check suitability.

Much of e-safety practice stems from a 2008 report, *Safer Children in a Digital World*, more commonly known as the Byron Review. This was one of the first studies to eschew the more emotive and polarised views on young people and digital technology, and concentrated on how parents and teachers could empower children to make safe and sensible decisions about the use of technology. Byron used a helpful framework in understanding young people's online behaviour, in drawing attention to how e-safety needed to be understood in terms of content (what children access and download), contact (whom they communicate with) and conduct (how they behave online) (Byron, 2008), and you may find that your own school's e-safety policy uses these terms. Certainly, Byron's (2010) 'Zip it, Block it, Flag it' code still provides a good starting point for discussions of online safety with pupils, as well as a useful code of practice.

Digital safety is now included as part of Ofsted's understanding of safeguarding within schools and in many ways as a direct response to the Byron Review, Ofsted published *The Safe Use of New Technologies* in 2010. Advocating a slight shift in educational practice, as well as following Byron's call to empower young learners, the report recommends that schools help pupils understand how to manage online risks, and to take informed responsibility for their own use of digital technology. The report argues that to achieve this, schools need to develop in three main areas: to develop a curriculum for e-safety, to provide training that enables all staff to support pupils, and to help families to keep their children safe. You may find that in your role as a TA you are involved in all three of these areas of activity.

As well as internet safety education programmes, online safety workshops and e-safety weeks, for example, online safety is now also firmly embedded into the National Curriculum, and depending on the context of your professional practice, it is essential that you are aware of the relevant DfE (2013) requirements for pupils:

> Key Stage 1 – use technology safely and respectfully, keeping personal information private; identify where to go for help and support when they have concerns about content or contact on the internet or other online technologies

> Key Stage 2 – use technology safely, respectfully and responsibly; recognise acceptable/unacceptable behaviour; identify a range of ways to report concerns about content and contact

> Key Stage 3 – understand a range of ways to use technology safely, respectfully, responsibly and securely, including protecting their online identity and privacy; recognise inappropriate content, contact and conduct, and know how to report concerns, and

> Key Stage 4 – understand how changes in technology affect safety, including new ways to protect their online privacy and identity, and how to report a range of concerns.

You may well find that e-safety is an area where you need further training and professional development. Remember that you are not alone here – in a more recent Ofsted report (2011), it was identified that staff training on issues of e-safety is a relative weakness in schools, particularly when responsibility for it has not been delegated. The report highlights how the provision of training is often not systematic, nor its impact monitored, and schools are still attempting to address this.

Assistive technology

Part of your role as a TA may be the dedicated support of pupils with special educational needs and disabilities (SEND), and as such, you may need to become familiar with a range of technologies that can be used to support their learning. These can range from basic devices (a pair of glasses, for example, can be seen as an assistive technology) and approaches such as the use of alternative fonts and different coloured paper and screen backgrounds, to more advanced software and hardware, such as screen magnification software, text-to-speech screen readers, alternative design keyboards and mice, and voice recognition software, which have been used in education for several years. More recently, research has been conducted on how children with Autism spectrum conditions respond well to technology, and particularly to robots, where they appear to serve as a prop during therapeutic sessions, and can make a potential contribution for both interacting with and supporting pupils.

The use of appropriate assistive technologies is a legal requirement for schools, and whilst the legislative frameworks for SEND are discussed in Chapter 10 of this book, their use is covered by the Equality Act (2010), where the responsible body for a school has a duty to make reasonable adjustments in support of a pupil's learning. Recent funding and administrative changes mean that schools must now use their best endeavours for children with SEND and they must have regard to the SEN Code of Practice. Historically, the selection and allocation of assistive technologies in schools have been based on what is termed as the medical model, where resources have been used according to a pupil's SEND. More recently, however, many have advocated a more child-centred approach – as McKnight and Davies (2012: 2) argue:

Considering assistive learning technologies from the point of view of the learners helps to identify approaches that are tailored to support specific impairments, as well as gaining greater understanding about issues facing learners with specific learning difficulties such as dyslexia, dyscalculia, dyspraxia, autistic spectrum disorders and ADHD, as well as physical disabilities such as visual or hearing impairments.

It is important to recognise that in the long term, the successful use of assistive technology may be as valuable and effective as your own support as a TA. You may be playing a key role in facilitating learning through supporting a learner through the use of assistive technology – this is crucial in both empowering the pupil and enabling them to become independent learners.

CASE STUDY 7.2

Sandeep

Sandeep is a secondary school pupil with dyslexia. In order to support her in her learning, the school has invested in Dragon Nuance, speech-to-text software that allows her to dictate to a PC when composing word-processing documents. Tim,

(continued)

(continued)

her class TA, has taught her how to use the software, and is now able to 'step back' in these sessions to allow Sandeep to approach her tasks independently. The school has only been able to afford to install the software on one PC, and the IT Technician has placed large signs on the wall, indicating that this is the PC with the software installed. Sandeep approaches Tim, saying that she feels embarrassed in using the software, and claiming that the signs make her feel very self-conscious. At this point it would be a good idea for Tim to talk to both the IT Technician and the SEN Co-ordinator, and have the signs removed. However well-meaning the IT Technician is being, it is important that learners are not further stigmatised in their use of assistive technology.

Chapter summary

Over the last 20 years or so, schools have invested heavily in technology, placing particular emphasis on infrastructure, leadership, resources and training. As the use of technology grows within schools, it is inevitable that the role of the TA will change to reflect this, with increasing use of both software and hardware in their day-to-day practice. This chapter has explored the context of the use of technology in schools and the role of the TA in this. Three important themes have also been discussed – the increasing use of new technologies such as web 2.0 tools and apps; the importance of e-safety; and how assistive technologies can support pupils with SEND. Identifying your own technological skills and training needs will be essential to successfully supporting pupils in their own use, as well as in other areas of your own professional practice. Such training will allow you to become more confident in your own use of technology, as well as being able to support pupils more effectively.

FURTHER READING

Buckingham, D. (2007) *Beyond technology: children's learning in an age of digital culture.* Cambridge: Polity.

Livingstone, S. (2009) *Children and the internet.* Cambridge: Polity.

Selwyn, N. (2010) *Schools and schooling in the digital age: a critical analysis.* London: Routledge.

Selwyn, N. (2014) *Distrusting educational technology: critical questions for changing times.* London: Routledge.

Selwyn, N. (2017) *Education and technology: key issues and debates* (2nd edn). London: Continuum.

Woollard, J. (2011) *Psychology for the classroom: e-learning.* London: Routledge.

References

Byron, T. (2008) *Safer children in a digital world: the report of the Byron Review*. Available at: http://media.education.gov.uk/assets/files/pdf/s/safer%20children%20in%20a%20 digital%20world%20the%202008%20byron%20review.pdf (Accessed: 17 March 2017).

Byron, T. (2010) *Do we have safer children in a digital world? A review of the progress since the 2008 Byron Review*. Available at: http://media.education.gov.uk/assets/files/ pdf/d/do%20we%20have%20safer%20children%20in%20a%20digital%20world%20 2010%20byron%20review.pdf (Accessed: 17 March 2017).

Davies, J. and Merchant, G. (2009) *Web 2.0 for schools: learning and social participation*. Oxford: Peter Lang.

Department for Education (DfE) (2013) *Statutory guidance: National Curriculum in England: computing programmes of study*. Available at: https://gov.uk/government/publications/ national-curriculum-in-england-computing-programmes-of-study/national-curriculum-in-england-computing-programmes-of-study (Accessed: 17 March 2017).

Equality Act (2010). Available at: http://legislation.gov.uk/ukpga/2010/15/pdfs/ukpga_ 20100015_en.pdf (Accessed: 17 March 2017).

Goodison, T. (2002) 'Learning with ICT at primary level: pupils' perceptions'. *Journal of Computer Assisted Learning*. Vol. 18, pp 282–295.

McKnight, L. and Davies, C. (2012) *Current perspectives on assistive learning technologies: 2012 review of research and challenges within the field*. Available at: http://kellogg.ox.ac. uk/sites/kellogg/files/Current%20Perspectives%20on%20Assistive%20Learning%20 Technologies.pdf (Accessed: 17 March 2017).

Morris, D. (2012) 'ICT and educational policy in the UK: are we on the way towards e-maturity or on the road to digital disaster?'. *Research in Teacher Education*. Vol. 2, No. 2, pp 3–8.

Ofsted (2009) *The importance of ICT: information and communication technology in primary and secondary schools, 2005/2008*. Available at: http://cnp.naace.co.uk/system/ files/The%20importance%20of%20ICT.pdf (Accessed: 17 March 2017).

Ofsted (2010) *The safe use of new technologies*. Available at: http://dera.ioe.ac.uk/1098/1/ The%20safe%20use%20of%20new%20technologies.pdf (Accessed: 17 March 2017).

Ofsted (2011) *ICT in schools 2008–11: an evaluation of information and communication technology education in schools in England 2008–11*. Available at: https://gov.uk/ government/uploads/system/uploads/attachment_data/file/181223/110134.pdf (Accessed: 17 March 2017).

Selwyn, N. (2006) 'Exploring the "digital disconnect" between net savvy students and their schools'. *Learning, Media and Technology*. Vol. 31, No. 1, pp 5–17.

Turvey, K., Potter, J., Allen, J. and Sharp, J. (2014) *Primary computing and ICT: knowledge, understanding and practice*. London: Sage.

8 Assessment and evaluation

Parminder Assi

CHAPTER OVERVIEW AND AIMS

- To explore the different purposes for assessing pupil learning

- To begin to understand and consider the differences between formative and summative assessment

- To consider how we can support assessments which are linked to learning and teaching in classrooms

- To begin to explore current debates about *what* is assessed by exploring 'success' criteria, data driven assessment and the regulation of learning through assessment

---

Introduction

This chapter will introduce you to a range of ideas exploring the use of assessment in education, how assessment affects the learning and teaching process, and the role of the TA. The chapter will focus on areas such as: why we assess, what is assessed and how assessment policy affects learning and teaching. The chapter will focus on four aspects; the integral role of assessment in learning and teaching, the differences between formative and summative assessment, assessment procedures and finally the effects of assessment on education. Throughout the chapter, you will be encouraged to reflect on your own observations, experiences and thoughts about the assessment process and how these may affect your work in the classroom. A range of examples will be used throughout the discussion as well as useful resources to support your understanding about the assessment of pupil learning. The research summaries offer an overview of work which can be followed up in more detail if needed and help you to make links between theory and practice.

TAs and their role in assessment

The origin of the word 'assess' derives from the Latin verb *assidere* ('to sit by'). This summarises the TA role well, in that TAs work closely with pupils and support learners on a daily basis. The TA supports assessment by making observations of what pupils know and understand, and then uses this information to plan for the next stage of learning. Using carefully planned learning activities, TAs work with pupils to guide learning, they make judgements of the progress made to record findings and share information with pupils, parents and colleagues. Bearing this in mind, the active involvement of both learner and TA illustrates well that assessment is 'at the heart of effective teaching' (Black and Wiliam, 1998: 2).

Although your role as the TA in assessment is generally closely linked to supporting individual pupils, it is likely that you are often involved in assessment practices which are not directly used to support individual learners. One example of this may be seen when pupils are supervised by TAs to practise responses to questions which have been used in formal assessments such as tests. TAs may find themselves managing the behaviour of pupils to ensure that they are on task rather than actively finding out how individuals engage with learning (in order to guide and support each pupil using their knowledge of both the learner and the learning content). The effectiveness of the TA role has therefore been affected by assessment which is focused on a need to prove that teaching support contributes to pupils achieving their set learning targets (Black *et al.*, 2002; 2003). We need to consider how to make assessment work for individual learners rather than to measure or grade how learners perform to a given set of expectations. In order to explore how the process of learning and assessment contributes to individual progress, we need to look at how specific types of assessment may be used to help the learner to move forward in learning.

REFLECTION POINTS

When I was in school my written work was marked with a cross or ticks (in red ink), at times there would be a written comment such as 'You have got a little behind', 'Poor' or 'See me'. I was left feeling confused and without guidance on what I should do next.

■ Reflect on the comment above from Kirsty.

■ What is feedback for?

(continued)

(continued)

- Consider the feedback you have been given on your own learning (or on the learning of others). What do you understand about the purpose of giving feedback to learners?

- What steps could be taken to ensure that assessment guides both the learner (and the teaching professional) to support progress?

In order to place assessment at the heart of the learning and teaching process we need to begin by exploring *how* and *why* assessment procedures and techniques are implemented.

Summative assessment

Summative assessment is used to monitor progress usually at the end of a term, topic or unit; this is often used to check grades and levels against assessment criteria. Summative assessment is often used to identify what students have learned set against criteria which is then graded. This information is then reported: examples include GCSEs, end-of-module tests, SATs and reading tests including the reading screen on phonics in England. Although summative assessment may describe what a student knows, understands and is able to do against a description or criteria (matched against a statement of achievement, much like a driving test which matches an individual's performance against set actions for operating a vehicle). However, these expectations may be linked to predetermined expectations or 'norm-referenced' (in the previous example used of the driving test, this may specify an age when all drivers are expected to pass the driving test). In schools, one example of how all learners are expected to reach a certain level at a set age can be found in the phonics screening used in England, here all pupils are expected to pass with a predetermined score at six years of age.

There are a number of concerns raised about the effects of summative assessment; however, the key focus here will be on formative assessment informally used by TAs to check progress made and support learners to the next stage of learning. One of the ways in which the TA role is integral to formative assessment is that TAs work closely with pupils and are able to build on the relationship that exists with their students. Given this close working relationship, TAs are able to focus on how individual pupils interpret information, how well they understand it, and how they can use it to make the next step in learning. TAs can readily gather information about the level of student engagement and use this information to make necessary changes during the learning in order to help guide progress. TAs make careful use of observation to gather information about the actual learning experience of the individual pupil, and this information is used to guide and support the pupil during the learning task.

CASE STUDY 8.1

Hayley

Hayley supports children with special educational needs in the classroom.

In one session we were using resources where the writing was quite small. After observing the pupil struggling to read the instructions, I showed the pupil how to use the magnifying sheet and helped the pupil write on a small whiteboard to guide the learning.

Think about the ways in which close observation of learners may be used to gain information on how the learner in engaging in learning.
  Think about a recent classroom teaching and learning activity.

■ What would you focus your observation on?

■ How would you use the information gained in order to guide subsequent planning and teaching?

Why is assessment an important topic?

A brief look at the historical context is necessary here in order to see how assessments have been designed for specific purposes and how decisions about the nature and content of the assessment have been arrived at. As we saw in Chapter 5, following the Education Reform Act (ERA) in 1988, a specification of what was to be taught (the National Curriculum) and a system of testing with the publication of results was implemented. This led to a strong focus on accountability as teaching staff were held to account if standards of pupil achievement fell below expectations. This use of assessment information was met with much concern and one of the responses was the setting up of a task group by the British Education Research Association (BERA) in 1989. This association aimed to investigate the importance of assessment on learning. Research led by the Assessment Reform Group (ARG) resulted in Black and Wiliam (1998) producing 'little books' summarising the importance of promoting assessment *for* learning (AfL) rather than assessment *of* learning. The authors called for a 'shift' in assessment, from 'testing' to 'assessment promoting learning' as it was noted that much of assessment in schools was about finding out how whole cohorts of learners were matching up to a set expectation or target, rather than assessment and feedback that would help individual learners to achieve in a variety of ways and at an individual pace.

How does assessment relate to learning theory?

Here we look at how the assessment of a learner's progress is integral to the learning and teaching process. To do so we need to look at the work of the psychologist Lev Vygotsky, who argued that learning is situated in a social context where pupils communicate their ideas and negotiate meanings by linking their learning to their social experiences. Vygotsky (1978) stated that language drives thinking and children use language to guide their understanding of what they are experiencing and to show their thinking. Learners also use language to organise steps in the learning process and to aid and communicate their ideas. Support is important as Vygotsky emphasised that learning is guided by a 'knowledgeable peer' or adult who is able to see where the pupil's understanding is (Vygotsky refers to this as the zone of proximal development, or ZPD). Knowing where the learner is in terms of 'learning steps' enables the TA to guide the learner to the next stage of learning. An example of this may be seen when we observe a child attempting to construct a jigsaw puzzle. Here, engaging the pupil in discussion, questioning them and carefully observing the attempts made at putting together the pieces of the jigsaw helps the TA to offer relevant guidance and support. When using this social constructivist model of learning we can see that both the learner and teaching staff are equally active and involved in the learning. This is because both the learner and the teacher have to observe, listen, communicate ideas and ask questions in order to complete the task in hand. These strategies help to make assessment integral and closely linked to the learning and teaching process and there are a range of procedures and techniques which can be used informally as formative assessment strategies to support learning.

Formative assessment procedures and techniques

Formative assessment describes the informal process of using assessment constantly alongside teaching and learning. This informal assessment is used throughout the school day to find out what learners can do and to give feedback to support progress. Wiliam (2011) describes the way in which both learners and teaching staff interact by constantly observing and making adjustments to learning to ensure that progress takes place. The first stage of a formative assessment is sharing learning aims, so that learners are aware of the purpose of the learning and how this relates to what they already know, understand and can do. The next stage of the formative assessment process is the shared activity of learning, as learners take ownership of their work, support other students in the learning process and engage with feedback on the progress they are making.

ACTIVITY

Read this quote from Nasir:

Formative assessment helps me to have a conversation about a topic, it allows discussion and identification of areas to be improved; it helps me to give regular feedback to a student throughout the lesson. I often ask open-ended questions and I use the learner's responses to help me guide and monitor the learning steps being taken.

■ Think of some examples of discussions and questioning you have seen being used in the classroom. How have these been used to guide children's understanding?

How can we plan for assessment?

When thinking about assessment, TAs should place learners at the centre of the planning and provide learners with an active role in the assessment process. Finding out about what a pupil already knows, understands and can do is important and this 'prior learning' can be used to guide plans by identifying and addressing 'gaps' in learning. TAs often share learning aims with learners in terms of expectations of what pupils will be doing and how a learning activity will help pupils to reach a specific goal. When planning such activities, you may think about the nature of support the learner may need during the task. You may also need to think about the subject knowledge needed to support an area of learning. Planning for the subject-specific knowledge, vocabulary and the key questions to ask during an activity can be written on a plan which may be annotated and adjusted in line with how you observe a pupil's progress. This information may be useful as a record to share with other colleagues when discussing the learner's progress.

CASE STUDY 8.2

Amy

Amy is a TA supporting a group of pupils ordering unit fractions in a mathematics class:

To begin most lessons, we start by asking the class open-ended questions that they are to answer in groups. They are given whiteboards to write their answers on and they are given five minutes to discuss the question in their groups. The

(continued)

(continued)

pupils were asked which of the following fractions was biggest: 1/6 or ½. One of the pupils stated:

'I think that 1/6 is bigger than ½.'

When I asked them why, the pupil replied:

'Because there is a big number on the bottom of the fraction.'

My role here was to show and explain (by using a pizza base) how the more parts there are, the smaller each portion will be.

Consider how you might plan to heighten the level of pupil engagement and discussion in learning, and engage pupils in more talk about their learning experiences. You may also look at how peer assessment helps students to focus on how they are learning as they share strategies they find useful with each other.

Assessment and use of questioning

TAs often report that pupils are passive in classrooms and do not generally start verbal interactions with teaching staff themselves. When questions are asked by teaching staff, these tend to be 'closed' questions, for example: *'How many tables are there in the classroom?'* This may serve to communicate to the child that there is only one 'correct' answer to a teacher-directed question. The use of 'open-ended' questioning such as *'Why do we have this number of tables in the classroom?'* helps to pose a challenge to learners and encourages them to engage in discussion. Open-ended questions also improve listening, concentration and confidence, and they boost learner ability in the sharing of ideas. It is important that pupils are encouraged to formulate questions themselves in order to find out the information they need, to move their learning on. Asking pupils to formulate questions and to think about what they will need to ask (so that they can locate relevant information) helps them to be involved and active, and encourages them to take responsibility for their own learning.

Learning about how we learn and metacognition

Through formative assessment, pupils can begin the process of finding out about how they themselves learn. This knowledge and awareness of how they learn is termed 'metacognition' (Flavell, 1979). The use of this knowledge about learning provides a means of making learners *proactive* rather than *reactive* in the learning process, as they begin to see how they can manage their own learning. One way of promoting metacognitive awareness is through the use of concept mapping. This is one way of involving pupils in recording what they know, understand and are able to do. At the beginning of an activity you may record with the learner what they already know about the specific area of learning selected. Following a series of learning activities, both you and the pupil can review the concept map and add to this in terms of how the learning has progressed. This way of mapping learning shows visually the progress made over a period of time and aids a process of self-assessment, informing the learner about their individual progress. Other strategies for self-assessment you may have used in classrooms includes 'traffic lights', 'thumbs up / thumbs down' etc. These strategies help to provide information to share pupils' experience of the learning task and encourages pupils to have ownership of and an active involvement in the assessment process.

CASE STUDY 8.3

Iram

Iram is a TA who has been using self-assessment and peer assessment in her classroom, as she describes:

> In my school, children are given a green pen to mark their own work and on occasions pass it to other students. They are beginning to self-assess using marking criteria to see how they can improve and where they need to focus their efforts.
>
> I often mark work throughout lessons; by doing this I am able to inform the students of what they have done well and give suggestions on how to improve so they are able to reach their learning objective. This helps the children with SEN, as quite often they view themselves as failures who are unable to get things right. By giving them ongoing, achievable advice, it helps to motivate them.
>
> We use a number of self-assessment techniques. I assist the students in comparing their work to the learning objective, which is often broken down into smaller, easier to understand objectives. We call this 'A wish and a star'. We encourage them to choose one objective they have achieved, naming this the 'star', and one objective they need to further improve, the 'wish'. We then discuss how they can improve in order to achieve their 'wish'.
>
> Reflect on the practice of sharing learning objectives with pupils in your setting.
>
> How could this be used so that pupils can specify their own 'success criteria' rather than having these criteria set?

Marking and feedback

It is important that where possible work is marked in collaboration with the learner. As you mark work with a pupil, think what would help the learner to make connections between what they can do and the next step. You may also focus on how the children managed the process and what they need do next.

Where possible feedback should be given *'in situ'* although it may also be written down; in the form of what was successfully done, how the work may be improved and what would be the next step in learning. It is important also to incorporate how the pupil managed the learning processes and not always focus on what they covered in terms of content and what they achieved as an outcome.

ACTIVITY

Ben, a TA, says:

> When I give feedback I want to encourage the pupils to build skills that will help them to become lifelong learners. So it is not just praising pupils for achieving, it is also to praise pupils for the skills they use to achieve, for example, perseverance, good noticing and collaboration.

■ Think about ways in which you might incorporate metacognition into your teaching in order to help pupils learn about their own individual ways of learning and the progress they have made.

Why are we concerned about assessment?

Much of the debate on assessment focuses on grave concerns about how summative assessment is affecting the nature of what is taught and how the teaching is done. Currently there have been a number of calls to re-evaluate the ways in which we assess; for example Morethanascore (2017) is a coalition of a diverse group of educational bodies including parents, teaching staff, educational psychologists and educational experts. This organisation campaigns for alternatives to the over-focus on summative assessment. In England concerns have also been raised about the assessment of the youngest of pupils (four-year-olds). Here, one 'baseline' assessment is administered in the first few weeks of starting school to all pupils, irrespective of their date of birth and diverse experiences prior to starting school. The use of these prescribed baseline assessment measures has influenced what teachers feel that they need to find out about a child's 'readiness' for learning (these being mostly related to literacy such as 'can write their own name'), (Assi and Reid, 2016). These early assessments of pupils have been responsible for fuelling low expectations through the labelling of pupils who do not meet set requirements (Bradbury and Roberts-Holmes, 2016).

There are many individual differences we need to consider when planning for assessment, including gender, special educational needs, pupils who may have English as an additional language, and wider individual differences between learners. In the same way that learners differ in their learning needs, they will also need different ways of showing what they can do. It is important to consider the use of a variety of assessment procedures and techniques and the different ways in which pupils can demonstrate their understanding. When we look at assessment, we can see that the score or result achieved by the learner will be affected by many factors. These factors include where the assessment takes place, the particular adult conducting the assessment, how familiar or strange the content of the assessment is and what the learner thinks the assessment is for. There may even be differences depending on what the child's home experiences have been and how these experiences may help (or hinder) 'expected' attainment. An example may be seen when we look at how many early assessments are conducted in the English language when we have many young children starting school who have English as an additional language.

How does assessment influence actions and attitudes?

Assessment has been compared to a system of surveillance because pupils (and teaching staff) are watched and monitored by their performance in assessments which are then evaluated and reported. Student scores are often passed on and compared to those from other schools in the form of comparative measures at a local, national and international level. It may be argued that assessment processes are used to encourage self-regulation and self-motivation (Broadfoot, 2007). Here we have the belief that assessment in school is a form of surveillance and self-regulation demonstrating a distribution of power. Both learners and teachers internalise what is expected of them in terms of targets to be reached. Foucault (1991) calls this a 'normalizing gaze', a form of 'self-surveillance' which engages assessment as a means of control and monitoring of individuals.

CASE STUDY 8.4

Assessment and TAs under the spotlight

Harry

As a teacher assistant having received countless observations, monitoring weeks and learning walks, I completely identify with the anxiety and stress that is caused by these processes – it creates imaginary surveillance in our minds; even if there are no observations scheduled, you never know if someone might come in.

(continued)

(continued)

Rusty

At the beginning of the year, with my Year 1 class, I was asked by a senior leader to predict which children would be age-related, above age-related or emerging into age-related at the end of Year 2. I was speechless, as from only having my class for approximately six weeks, how was I possibly able to make a clear judgement for over a year's time? I automatically picked the ones I knew I could move easily, when in fact having thought about it, why should the education of a class of 30 children come down to picking just five in an office, during one stressful meeting? But then how can I question a headteacher who also has the pressure of making sure that the SATs results are better than last year's and to make an effect on the league tables, to keep Ofsted at bay, and to also to keep his job and ours?

Think about how learning is managed and organised in your setting (what is taught, when and how it is taught and how the learners are grouped etc). What messages does this signal about what is seen as important and valuable in learning?

Concerns have been raised about how classes scheduled to take national tests spend more time and energy rehearsing how to pass these test. This often means that there is less time to actually develop pupils' skills and understanding in lessons like art, PE and music, which often take a back seat. Along with effects on the curriculum, the effects of this approach to assessment has also affected student's self-esteem. Reay and Wiliam (1999) show how assessments such as SATs significantly reduce learner confidence, often resulting in a self-disparaging attitude. Evidence submitted to the Morethanascore organisation (2017) shows that English children are amongst some of the unhappiest in the world, increasing the likelihood of unstable mental health.

Chapter summary

In this chapter we have established that assessment is an important part of learning and teaching and it should be linked closely to the ongoing daily interaction between learners and TAs. The use of formative assessment helps learners become actively involved in their learning, as pupils are encouraged to take responsibility for their own learning by being involved in assessment and making choices about how best they can show what they know, understand and can do. In the same way in which learners differ in their learning approaches and preferences they should also have opportunities to show what they can do, by having access to a variety of diverse assessment methods including self-assessment.

Teamwork and co-operation between colleagues and the home context is important for effective learning, teaching and assessment to take place. By sharing observations and feedback from a variety of different contexts TAs can move learners forward in their learning. Monitoring, record-keeping and reporting of assessment are important aspects of the TA's role in schools; however, TAs also need to be mindful of the effects of assessment on their work, on their pupils and on what is seen as worthwhile and valuable in learning.

FURTHER READING

Assessment Reform Group (2002) *Assessment for learning: 10 principles. Research based principles to guide classroom practice.* Available at: https://aaia.org.uk/blog/2010/06/16/assessment-reform-group/ (Accessed: 15 March 2018).

Morethanascore (2017) *More than a score.* Available at: https://morethanascore.co.uk/ (Accessed: 25 September 2017)

References

Assi, P. and Reid, S. (2016) 'Baseline assessments: what teachers say about assessing young children on entry to primary school'. *Education Journal.* Vol. 281, pp 17–19.

Black, P. and Wiliam, D. (1998) *Inside the black box: raising standards through classroom assessment.* London: School of Education, Kings College (reissued by NFER Nelson, 2004).

Black, P., Harrison, C., Lee, C., Marshall, B. and Wiliam, D. (2002) *Working inside the black box: assessment for learning in the classroom.* London: Kings College, London.

Black, P., Harrison, C., Lee, C., Marshall, B. and Wiliam, D. (2003) *Assessment for learning: putting it into practice.* Maidenhead: Open University Press.

Bradbury, A. and Roberts-Holmes, G. (2016) *The introduction of reception baseline assessment: 'They are children. . . not robots, not machines'.* London: ATL and NUT. Available at: http://teachers.org.uk/files/baseline-assessment--final-10404.pdf (Accessed: 28 November 2016).

Broadfoot, P. (2007) *An introduction to assessment.* London: Continuum.

Flavell, J.H. (1979) 'Metacognition and cognitive monitoring: a new area of cognitive-developmental inquiry'. *American Psychologist.* Vol. 34, No. 10, pp 906–911.

Foucault, M. (1991) *Discipline and punish: the birth of the prison.* London: Penguin.

Morethanascore (2017) *More than a score.* Available at: https://morethanascore.co.uk/ (Accessed: 20 October 2017).

Reay, D. and Wiliam, D. (1999) '"I'll be a nothing": structure, agency and the construction of identity through assessment.' *British Educational Research Journal.* Vol. 25, No. 3, pp 343–354.

Vygotsky, L. (1978) *Mind in society.* Cambridge, MA: Harvard University Press.

Wiliam, D. (2011) *Embedded formative assessment.* London: Hawker Brownlow Education.

PART III
Supporting pupils' learning needs

9 Working with families

Jacky Taylor

CHAPTER OVERVIEW AND AIMS

- To explore our concerns around working with families

- To help you begin to think about developing a shared setting philosophy and active culture to influence your vision of working with families

- To help you consider how parents might act when agencies present values different from their own

- To find and use ideas to support good practice based on your individual setting's needs

- To discover ways to share good practice and evaluate next steps for you and your setting

Introduction

The aim of this chapter is to help you understand the importance of parental partnerships and is written for anyone working with children from age four to age 18. Parental partnerships need to be active and involve ongoing participation of a parent or primary caregiver in the education of his or her child. Schools with involved parents engage those parents and incorporate them into the learning process. Firstly, please do not underestimate the role you play in helping to make learning valuable within a whole family process to support the child's learning journey. This is because effective parental partnerships cannot be conceptualised simply by the use of specific strategies such as parenting programmes or styles; parents change their approaches to parenting as the need arises, as should we. Your role may well be the one that parents feel is accessible. Parents know that you know their child.

To begin it would be helpful to consider our concerns around working with families and firstly put issues into perspective. Social scientists give value to the role parents play in the family structure, agreeing that actions of parents can affect the environment and circumstances in which a child grows. In an intriguing piece of research, Desforges and Abouchaar (2003: 15) reasoned that the types of research used at the time to gather data on settings working with families confused the complexities of examining the role of the parent, arguing, 'The design of most early studies did not allow these complex relations amongst variables to be unpicked to identify their unique effects'.

What we can draw from their research, and what Desforges and Abouchaar argued, is that what parents do with their children, including at home, is of greater significance than any other factor open to educational influence. This connects well to the work of Bronfenbrenner (1979) who argued family experience has a profound influence on life chances, meaning that wherever the family are, whether in the home or attending groups within a school setting, it is the shared experience and not necessarily the venue or anticipated outcome that affects the learning and hence the life chances of the child. This is where you and your setting come in: by creating welcoming, non-judgmental environments, a whole family experience – managed well – will make a difference to the family and ultimately the child.

CASE STUDY 9.1

A Year 2 parent

I wanted to know what my son does in Year 2. He is a quiet lad and when I ask him what he has done that day he says: 'Not much, work, you know'. He's at that age now when I'm expected to drop him at the gate and not get involved. But I want to. I want to know if I am helping him as well. Parents' evening is OK, but what can I find out in a ten-minute meeting with a queue of parents sat next to me looking at their watches because they want to be home for Coronation Street?

REFLECTION POINTS

- What is your reaction to the parent's comment above?

- How could this setting improve the parent's relationship with the school?

- How does your setting currently work with parents?

- Do you feel it is effective?

- What are the barriers to effective parental engagement?

After considering the case study and reflecting, we now need to consider how schools and settings that are already struggling with overcrowded timetables find time to build productive partnerships with parents and carers. We also need to reflect on why at the end of a Year 9 parents' evening, when the attendance figures are checked we often hear 'Same old thing, the ones you really need to see never turn up! Hard-to-reach parents again!' It is important to consider why some parents choose to avoid engaging with their child's setting.

Hard-to-reach families

Within the education sector working with families has a two-pronged focus: parental involvement with children's learning and promoting positive, pro-social behaviour (Allen and Duncan-Smith, 2008: 91). The preamble to the Teachers' Standards (DfE, 2012) states teachers should work with parents in the best interests of their pupils. This importance of parental engagement was also recognised by the Ofsted framework, which required inspectors to consider the extent to which leadership within schools 'engages with parents and carers in supporting pupils' achievement, behaviour and safety and their spiritual, moral, social and cultural development' (Ofsted, 2012).

Family identity appears to be complex and membership of this group is made up of a combination of factors such as social class, gender, single parent status, ethnicity, postcode and prior learning. Although various studies have led to definitions of their characteristics and behaviours, it is important to note that there is not one single factor which determines the nature of a 'hard-to-reach family'. A definition by Levitas (1998) summed it up well, defining hard-to-reach as those who are socially excluded and who need to be re-engaged as stakeholders. These stakeholders have become a target of many interventions and we do have a growing awareness of the potential impact of families on both educational attainment and progression into further and higher education.

Crozier and Davies (2007) suggested it is schools themselves that inhibit accessibility for certain parents rather than the parents themselves being hard to reach. In their two-year study on home-school relationships, they cite Bernstein (1975) who studied how the structure of social relationships influences the structure of communication, and how the structure of communication shapes people's consciousness and identity – through the curriculum. Crozier and Davies assert that schools adopt what might be seen as middle class values; meaning school expectation renders certain types of parents as invisible in terms of what they can bring to the school or offer. You now need to consider what your setting currently offers or how they support those families who do not attend regularly. You then need to reflect on the impact of how the parent in the case study might stop engaging if they do not feel included in their child's learning journey. By using the reflection points we can begin to consider this further.

CASE STUDY 9.2

A Year 9 teacher

It's really difficult to work with hard-to-reach families. They don't engage with the school and you never see them unless you call them in for a meeting to talk about their child's behaviour or progress. Often you send a letter and they don't attend and then they wonder why at parents' evening their son or daughter gets a rubbish report.

REFLECTION POINTS

■ How do you feel about the teachers' comments above?

■ What do these comments say about the school's relationship with the family?

■ Does your school use the term 'hard-to-reach families'?

If so, think about the families you associate with this description.

- ■   Why are they called this?

- ■   Are these families hard to reach or hard to engage with?

- ■   What strategies have you tried so far?

- ■   What has worked and what hasn't worked?

A precise definition of what a hard-to-reach family looks like without knowing their specific circumstances or the context they live within is hard to achieve. A research report by Campbell (2011) argues some school leaders suggest there are certain characteristics that hard-to-reach groups or those who do not engage share, such as being a mixture of the unemployed, those experiencing a low income, having English as a second language, being parents of poor attendees or being non-responsive to contact. Campbell (2011: 10) argues that 'hard-to-reach' is more about families who 'have very low levels of engagement with school, do not attend school meetings nor respond to communications and who exhibit high levels of inertia in overcoming perceived barriers to participation'. The use of the term 'non-responsive' could imply there is something wrong with the parent and that non-engagement with the school is not a fault of the school but rather the family; already we are considering a deficit approach to family work.

Same values, different perspectives?

So far within this chapter we have begun considering our own attitudes to the parents and families who do not access services or make contact with us and have considered developing a shared setting philosophy with the aim of engaging families. We also need to begin to consider the school experience from the perspective of the family.

Everyone brings values, principles, attitudes and beliefs with them in their personal and professional life. Values are the moral principles and beliefs guiding individuals and social, ethnic or cultural groups to behave in certain ways. Values inform choices about what is good or acceptable and what is viewed as bad or unacceptable. They also allow us all to prioritise what is more or less important. Values shape our behaviour and what we decide to do in different situations; our values are the things we care about (Ghaye, 2011: 30). When parents send their children to school, some may breathe a sigh of relief, whilst others who have spent a great deal of time selecting their child's school, sense the start of shifting roles; from being their child's only and first teacher they may consider what it will be like to be part of the team now the child is at school and how this new partnership will help their child.

When schools receive children, they may have similar thoughts to the parents. Some staff set about developing the shared role of educating the children, devising ways to co-operatively work together with families; some breathe a sigh of relief when the parents have left the premises, as they can now get on with what they feel is their job – educating the child. As a result, for many children home and school rarely overlap. At points of transition (recruiting children, choosing options and leaving school) these worlds may collide, often during the same parents' evening mentioned previously. Many schools have meetings across the year to discuss 'progress' with a parent sitting on a child-sized chair and a teacher sitting on an adult-sized seat, looking down and talking from a position of power.

REFLECTION POINTS

■ Should these positions of power be allowed to happen?

■ Consider how the seating situation might impact on the parent's engagement within the discussion.

■ If the seating arrangements were reversed, how this would make us (staff), feel?

However, it need not be a tale of two separate worlds and it is possible to develop real partnerships and shared values between the school, the child and the family. These partnerships and values need meaningful interactions, between the setting/school and the home, and a shared ethos or philosophy needs to be felt by the school and family alike. As already mentioned these begin initially with breaking down the barriers to effective parental engagement.

CASE STUDY 9.3

A parent's own schooldays

I hated school myself, we moved to the area half way through my first term in Year 1. I can still remember the other kids ignoring me and not playing with me. I cried a lot and told my Mum I didn't want to go to school. She used to shout at me and tell me school was nothing to do with her and I had to go. I don't remember Mum ever coming up to the school to tell them I was upset.

REFLECTION POINTS

■ What might the impact of this situation be in the long term on the child?

■ What could you have done to explore this situation and support the parent and ultimately the child to build trusting relationships?

■ How do you and your setting welcome new families to the setting/school?

■ What needs to happen first in building this relationship with the school/setting?

In 2012 Fothergill produced a report in conjunction with the CBI in which he suggested schools should go beyond the academic into the behaviours and attitudes of families and adopt strategies for supporting parental engagement and wider community involvement. This would form the basis for the development of new policies and procedures for engagement. This means that when reflecting on how we work with families we must consider that no two settings/schools are staffed by the same people or have the same parents and families. We need to get to know 'our' families, what they want (not what we think they need) and try to respond to their individual needs.

To combat any preconceived perceptions of what families want or need, lessons can be learned by putting yourself in the family's shoes. Consider how parents might feel when they are asked by the school to engage in something potentially new or challenging for them; for example listening to a Year 1 child read at home or ensuring a Year 9 child has space and time for revision and homework. As practitioners we need to ensure families want to engage and stop families feeling excluded from the territory that was once theirs, educating their child. We need to reflect and try to understand the potential barriers to parental engagement in the process.

Developing an active culture of working with families, including dads

We need in our practice to consider parental self-esteem or, as Bandura (1986) described, parental self-efficacy or self-belief; in other words when parents feel they can make a positive contribution to their own child's learning. Melhuish *et al.* (2008: 1641) suggested parents with strong self-efficacy are more likely to become involved in their child's education, through choice. This is a concept we need to reflect upon and develop if possible; parents may have had a negative experience of school themselves and this may cloud their opinion and confidence in their engagement in the school. Unless we discover whether this is the case, we cannot encourage them to move away from those experiences and develop strong links to support their own child's learning and development. Previous experience of school can produce negative memories for some parents. Parents were once children themselves and may have encountered bullying, low achievement, exclusion, family hardship to name but a few circumstances.

The issue of gender also needs to be considered in ensuring equality and support for all parents. When you consider working with families, it is easy to picture mothers, but do you work just as hard to involve fathers? Research indicates children benefit from higher academic achievement and social and emotional well-being if their fathers are involved in their education (Morgan *et al.*, 2009: 167). This also supports the strong messages from Blewett (2008), who argued we should not make assumptions about fathers and should work to counter any negative perceptions by making services in schools male-friendly.

Settings must also reflect on how they include absent fathers who do not regularly see their children, fathers who only see their children at weekends and therefore do not have contact with the school, working fathers who do not drop off or pick up their children, men attempting to fit into home-learning practices already established by mothers, such as reading and helping with homework, and finally issues created by gender role modelling, particularly within primary schools where the majority of staff are women and fathers feel less confident in voicing their worries and concerns. Lewis and Lamb (2007) researched literature on fathering itself and concluded that fatherhood has a complex, interrelated relational and economic role often polarised into stereotypical opinions of the role of fathers from Supermen to deadbeats by staff and settings.

Existing roles and responsibilities in our work can create work demands or boundaries we never cross, such as issues of not having enough time to make significant changes to working practices and who is responsible for communication and organising additional events. Reflecting on these boundaries or tensions and taking steps towards resolving them must be undertaken if working with families is to be effective. By developing strong working groups in the school, jobs seem a little smaller and take up a little less time – just like the old saying: many hands make light work. Equally it is important for school leaders to understand the constraints on staff of working with families. Talk to the senior staff in the school, voice your ideas, tell them you want to develop this area of working either yourself or by supporting someone else to undertake it and involve them in the process.

ACTIVITY

- Look at the policy of your setting on working with parents; is there specific mention of fathers/male carers?

- Organise a focus group for all staff to share their thoughts on working with families to create some excitement for developing a shared philosophy in your setting.

- Ask parents how your setting can try to overcome barriers to participation.

A toolkit of ideas/strategies

Develop a toolkit of strategies you can use to improve parental engagement, such as the following.

- Home visits are seen as one of the most effective means of working with hard-to-reach families (McAuley *et al.*, 2006).

- Offer parenting courses to build confidence and address any underlying issues (if they exist) around behaviour.

- Develop 'Dads groups', making things, repairing bird-feeding stations etc.

- Communicating – how does your setting communicate with parents/families? As well as the more formal approaches such as newsletters and school websites, use informal communication methods such as current technology: send texts; use social media: set up (or even better, ask a parent to set up) a parents' Facebook page where they can ask the questions they might be too afraid to ask the school.

- Encourage volunteering – it may be your school has a no-parent-in-classroom policy, but what else could they be involved with? Are there any jobs around school that parents could help with, such as gardening or building bird feeders for the children?

- Arrange family learning courses – research your parents, don't always assume literacy levels are high, and develop some workshops aimed at supporting specific year groups, homework help or study guides.

- Provide opportunities for decision-making – how can families influence the setting, as governors or members of a parent teacher association? Could your school develop a parents' council, useful for those parents to approach if parents work long hours or away from home and can't get into school within school hours?

- Collaborate with the community – ask parents what needs to be done in the local community and try and organise a working group to come up with some ideas.

Chapter summary

Working with families is not easy, but it is achievable if you persist and involve key stakeholders such as the school leadership team and of course the parents themselves. School leaders should develop an ethos of communication with all their parents, and focus on those parents/carers who are hard to engage. If you show a willingness to learn more about your pupils from their parents, then they will be more willing to work with you. To do this you need to be prepared to listen to what parents have to say, show an interest in them and remember the influences in their own life that may have encouraged them to feel the way they do about education in general and their role in their children's learning.

Your goal is to provide a link between the school and home. Parents need to feel comfortable and can become a critical friend to the school, providing their time and enthusiasm to reap rewards not achieved in isolation. Parents bring skills and knowledge and successful schools 'are those where parental engagement is at the centre of the school ethos as opposed to being at the periphery' (Campbell, 2011: 37). Staff and particularly those supporting children and young people in schools must conceive of themselves as agents of change rather than victims of change (Johnson and Hallgarten, 2002). This requires a change in mindset to one where you engage authoritatively with social justice (Cunningham, 2008) and view families as stakeholders capable of grasping and shaping opportunities and value your role within interventions, developing quality practice in working together.

In ending this chapter I return to the research of Desforges and Abouchaar (2003) who argued parents need to be involved in their children's learning process. As discussed, interventions should have a clear developmental focus; this way there is more opportunity to build a positive set of home-school relationships and remove obstacles to the acquisition of capability. Development between family and setting should be ongoing, as families have sensitive periods during which they are particularly responsive to different types of interventions. School-based education alone is insufficient in supporting children's learning (Lindsay et al., 2011) and working with families should be embedded in every setting's teaching and learning strategy and development plans; as without a strategic approach to change, involving families in supporting children's learning will remain ad-hoc with little evaluation and subsequent planned improvement.

FURTHER READING

National Occupational Standards – Work with Parents (2011). Available at: http://dera.ioe. ac.uk/2024/1/work-with-parents-nos-jan-2011.pdf (Accessed: 15 March 2018). This framework provides an excellent springboard to working with families and specifically parents. It provides evidence to support a case for extending work in your school.

Allen, G. and Duncan-Smith, I. (2008) *Early intervention: good parents, great kids, better citizens.* London: Centre for Social Justice.

Campbell, C. (2011) *How to involve hard-to-reach parents: encouraging meaningful parental engagement with schools.* Nottingham: National College for School Leadership. Available at: http://dera.ioe. ac.uk/12136/1/download%3Fid%3D156367%26filename%3Dhow-to-involve-hard-to-reach-parents-full-report.pdf (Accessed: 15 March 2018).

Cunningham, B. (2008) *Exploring professionalism.* London: Institute of Education, University of London.

References

Allen, G. and Duncan-Smith, I. (2008) *Early intervention: good parents, great kids, better citizens.* London: Centre for Social Justice.

Bandura, A. (1986) 'The explanatory and predictive scope of self-efficacy theory'. *Journal of Clinical and Social Psychology.* Vol. 4, pp 359–373.

Bernstein, B. (1975) *Class codes and control*, Vol 111. London: Routledge and Kegan Paul.

Blewett, J. (2008) 'Fatherhood and parenting: messages from research'. *Community Care.* May 2008.

Bronfenbrenner, U. (1979) *The ecology of human development.* Cambridge, MA: Harvard University Press.

Campbell, C. (2011) *How to involve hard-to-reach parents: encouraging meaningful parental engagement with schools.* Nottingham: National College for School Leadership.

Crozier, G. and Davies, J. (2007) 'Hard to reach parents or hard to reach schools? A discussion of home-school relations, with particular reference to Bangladeshi and Pakistani parents'. *British Educational Research Journal.* Vol. 33, No. 3, pp 295–313.

Cunningham, B. (ed.) (2008) *Exploring professionalism.* London: Institute of Education, University of London.

Desforges, C. and Abouchaar, A. (2003) *The impact of parental involvement, parental support and family education on pupil achievement and adjustment.* Research Report 433. London: DfES.

Department for Education (DfE) (2012) *Teachers Standards.* Available at: https://education.gov. uk/publications/eOrderingDownload/teachers%20standards.pdf (Accessed: 20 July 17).

Fothergill, J. (2012) *First steps: a new approach for our schools.* London: CBI.

Ghaye, T. (2011) *Teaching and learning through reflective practice.* Abingdon: Routledge.

Johnson, M. and Hallgarten, J. (eds) (2002) *From victims of change to agents of change: the future of the teaching profession.* London: Institute for Public Policy Research.

Levitas, R. (1998) *The inclusive society? Social exclusion and New Labour*. London: Macmillan.

Lewis, C. and Lamb, E. (2007) *Understanding fatherhood: a review of recent research*. York: Joseph Rowntree Foundation.

Lindsay, G., Cullen, S. and Wellings, C. (2011) *Bringing families and schools together: giving children in high-poverty areas the best start at school*. London: Save the Children.

McAuley, C., Pecora, P.J. and Rose, W. (eds) (2006) *Enhancing the well-being of children and families through effective interventions*. London: Jessica Kingsley.

Melhuish, E., Belsky, J., Leyland, A. and Barnes, J. (2008) 'Effects of fully established SureStart local programmes on 3-year-old children and their families living in England: a quasi-experimental observational study'. *The Lancet*. Vol. 372, pp 1641–1647.

Morgan, A., Nutbrown, C. and Hannon, P. (2009) 'Fathers' involvement in young children's literacy development: implications for family literacy programmes'. *British Educational Research Journal*. Vol. 35, No. 2, pp 167–185.

Ofsted (2012) *The evaluation schedule for the inspection of maintained schools and academies*. Available at: http//ofsted.gov.uk/resources/framework-for-school-inspection-september-2012-0 (Accessed: 20 July 17).

Special educational needs, disability and inclusion

Clare Bright

CHAPTER OVERVIEW AND AIMS

- To explore definitions of inclusion and the characteristics of inclusive learning and teaching

- To gain an understanding of the legislation for SEND and how schools put policy into practice

- To understand some of the challenges for learners with SEND

- To evaluate a number of strategies to support pupils with SEND including the role of the TA

- To provide links to resources on a number of special educational needs and disabilities

Introduction

Provision in schools for children and young people with Special Educational Needs and Disabilities (SEND) is likely to be a significant part of your role in school. In this chapter we explore some of the challenges you might face in meeting the needs of pupils with SEND and their families. The chapter begins with definitions of inclusion and you will be introduced to models of disability. You will be provided with an overview of the legislation for SEND and how this supports pupils with SEND. We will discuss some of the challenges for learners with SEND and consider how schools can promote inclusive learning and teaching.

You will be encouraged to evaluate strategies to support pupils with SEND, including the role of the TA. At the end of the chapter there will be a list of useful resources and links to information on a range of SEND.

What is meant by inclusion?

As a practitioner in a school setting you are sure to be familiar with the term 'inclusion' but if asked to define it, what would you say? Ainscow, Dyson and Booth (2006) distinguish between a 'broad' and a 'narrow' view of inclusion and to begin we will explore the difference.

A broad definition of inclusion is one that considers *all* learners and recognises learner diversity and learner differences. Within this we can recognise distinct groups of children, some of whom can find education challenging. The reasons for these challenges can be due to a number of factors and could include some of those listed below that you might not have considered before:

- Pupils with English as an additional language (see Chapter 12)

- Pupils with SEND

- Traveller children

- Looked after children

- Asylum seekers

- Recently bereaved children or young people

- Children living in poverty

- More able pupils

- LGBT pupils

It impossible to list all the factors here and you are bound to be able to add to this list for yourself. What this demonstrates, however, is that there are many children in individual circumstances which may make them what is sometimes termed 'vulnerable' or at risk of being excluded from education. This does not necessarily mean they are not allowed to attend school but it might indicate that there are practices in schools that are 'exclusionary' for some pupils and demonstrate discrimination or 'intolerance to difference' (Booth and Ainscow, 2011: 43). Those children who are disaffected from education and are sometimes viewed as 'problems' are discussed further in Chapter 11.

A narrower interpretation of inclusion is one that focuses on specific groups of pupils, mainly those with special educational needs and disabilities (SEND). To help us to understand inclusion more effectively it is useful first to consider the two most common models of disability.

Models of disability

The medical model of disability is seen as a deficit model that defines people with disabilities by their impairment and focuses on what they are not able to do rather than on what they can do. The emphasis is put on making the disabled person 'better' or 'fixing' them by finding ways to help them to become more 'normal' in the belief that this will improve their quality of life. This model expects the disabled person to change in order to fit into society. The use of the term 'normal' here emphasises that this model views difference between people as a disadvantage rather than something to be celebrated.

The social model of disability, however, recognises that disability stems from barriers created by society rather than situating the problem with the disabled person. These barriers might be environmental, institutional or attitudinal. This model identifies that it is the responsibility of society to remove the barriers, allowing disabled people to be independent and equal in society, with choice and control over their own lives (Scope, 2017). Although widely recognised as significant in altering perceptions of people with disabilities it has been argued that this model fails to appreciate individual differences and regards people with disabilities as one homogenous group (Hodkinson, 2016). It has also been suggested that by putting all their difficulties down to society, it erodes the individual lived experience of those with a disability.

Definitions of 'inclusion'

As a concept, inclusion is complex and there are multiple definitions. For many, inclusion refers to *where* a pupil is educated which has a historical legacy and stems from the practice of segregating pupils with SEND or 'handicapped' pupils from 'normal' pupils when formerly they were often viewed as 'uneducable'. The language used here may seem shocking to us now but it is what was commonly used before the late 1970s and reflects some of the attitudes around disability that were prevalent at that time.

Baroness Warnock is usually attributed with making the first attempts to recognise the needs of children with learning difficulties and disabilities in her report of 1978. Warnock (1978) referred to the term 'special educational needs' and promoted the practice of educating children, whatever their disabilities, with their peers in mainstream settings rather than separating them into special school settings. However, as mentioned earlier, the practice of educating children together may be described as inclusive but inclusive practice goes beyond where children are located for their education. Although children with special needs and disabilities were present in mainstream schools there was an expectation that the children would adapt in order to fit into the school or to become integrated into the school community. Since Warnock's initial report she has clarified that the expectation of the original recommendations was to provide more effectively for children with moderate learning difficulties already in mainstream schools, thus enabling more children to be taught in mainstream settings. The original report did not suggest that this would be the case for all children but this is how it was interpreted at the time.

Another definition of inclusion refers to the rights of children to have an equal education. This was promoted by the Salamanca Statement of 1994 which was agreed by 92 nations and stated that it should be the right of all children to be educated in normal schools. Once again the language used is ambiguous and we are forced to question if 'normal' schools equate to what we understand as mainstream schools. The 'rights-based' view of inclusion is one that links back to the social model of disability and places an expectation clearly on schools to make appropriate whole-school changes in order to provide effectively for all children, whatever their needs and difficulties.

Inclusion is often associated with equality of opportunity. This has to be considered carefully and it must be understood that this does not mean treating everyone the same. We know that for many reasons education is not equal and yet it is the job of schools to provide pupils with opportunities that are equal. This might mean that steps must be taken to ensure pupils can access the same educational possibilities as everyone else, which is addressed in the following section on the legislation in place for SEND. This might be a major aspect of your role in school.

Other definitions of inclusion refer to it as a process and they suggest that settings need to engage in evolving their policies and practices to enable participation for all pupils. Some definitions refer to pupils feeling that they belong to the school community and are valued. Others suggest that inclusion can only be achieved if schools undergo cultural transformation and consider their curriculum, relationships, organisation and pedagogy in order to serve their community appropriately.

SEND legislation

The *Special educational needs and disability code of practice: 0 to 25 years* is the document that explains the duties of local authorities, health bodies, schools and colleges in England to provide for pupils with SEND under part 3 of the Children and Families Act 2014. The SEND Code of Practice 2015 is underpinned by a number of key principles which are referred to throughout. There is a strong emphasis on involving the child/young person and the family in the decision-making and taking their views into account. The Code expects professionals to provide high-quality teaching that is differentiated to meet the needs of individuals. For children who make less than expected progress and are identified as requiring SEN support, it suggests a four-part cycle of assess, plan, do, review. If the interventions provided by the school through their notional SEN budget still do not enable the child to meet agreed outcomes, the school or parent can request an Education, Health and Care needs assessment. If successful, this will lead to additional funding from the LEA to support the child through an Education, Health and Care plan.

The definition of SEND from the Code of Practice states that 'a child or young person has SEN if they have a learning difficulty or disability which calls for special educational provision to be made for him or her' (DfE, 2015: 15) The legislation recognises four broad areas of need but recognises that some children will have needs that cross over more than one category and may change over time (DfE, 2015: 97):

■ communication and interaction

■ cognition and learning

■ social, emotional and mental health

■ sensory and/or physical needs.

Another important point of reference in England and Wales is the Equality Act 2010 which states that a person has a disability if it has a substantial and long-term adverse effect on the person's ability to carry out normal day-to day activities (Equality Act, 2010: 6). The Act clarifies the responsibilities of school leaders and government to avoid discrimination and promote equality for all pupils, regardless of their circumstances and backgrounds. The Act extends to schools' admissions policies and also states that pupils with disabilities must not be placed at a disadvantage relative to a person who is not disabled. In this regard settings are required to make 'reasonable adjustments' to ensure that any potential disadvantage is removed. We consider a number of reasonable adjustments and strategies to support SEND later in this chapter.

The role of the SENCO

The SEND Code of Practice 2015 identifies that all schools must have a Special Educational Needs Co-ordinator (SENCO) who is required to be a qualified teacher. It suggests that they will be most effective in that role if they are a member of the school leadership team. The requirement of the SENCO to gain additional qualifications to carry out this role is discussed in Chapter 14. The SENCO has a number of key responsibilities and should be given time in order to carry out their functions.

ACTIVITY

■ Talk to the SENCO in your setting to find out what their key responsibilities are.

■ Look at the school website for the school SEN policy and school offer.

■ How is information on the children with SEND communicated to staff?

■ What opportunities are there for staff to discuss provision for pupils with SEND in your setting?

Challenges for pupils with SEND

There is insufficient space within this chapter to look at different needs and disabilities in depth, so it is the aim of this section to identify some of the more common barriers to learning that result from having a special need or disability. These are categorised under the broad areas of need identified in the SEND Code of Practice 2015. It is important to recognise that some children may have more than one condition at the same time, which is known as comorbidity.

Communication and interaction

Children with speech, language and communication difficulties may struggle to understand what is said to them, have difficulty in saying what they want to say, or they may not understand or use the social rules of communication. Children and young people with ASD, Asperger's Syndrome and Autism are included in this category of need as they may have difficulty with some or all of the aspects of communication mentioned above but also with imagination and how they relate to others.

Social, emotional and mental health

In the previous Code of Practice of 2001 the equivalent category of need included behavioural difficulties. The current Code has removed this and explains that teachers need to establish the reason for a pupil's behavioural difficulties before attributing them to having a SEND. The reason for this was that there had been over-identification of behavioural difficulties that teachers should be able to manage without the need for additional intervention (Frederickson and Cline, 2015). The recognition of mental health difficulties in the legislation reflects the significant increase in the numbers of children and young people who display behaviours that might reflect underlying mental health difficulties. These include anxiety, depression, self-harming, substance misuse and eating disorders. Attention deficit disorder, attention deficit hyperactive disorder or attachment disorders are also included in this category. Managing pupil behaviour is discussed in Chapter 11.

Sensory and/or physical needs

For some pupils with physical difficulties mobility can be a challenge. Moving around the building to access specialist teaching spaces and outside spaces must be considered. Pupils with sensory impairments which include visual and hearing impairments can struggle with the classroom environment, noise and light levels which can impact on their ability to see, hear and concentrate. In themselves physical difficulties do not limit learning but if the pupil is denied learning opportunities or has to work extra hard to learn, this will have an impact.

Cognition and learning

Learning and cognitive needs vary from mild to severe and usually mean that a pupil will learn at a slower pace than their peers. Moderate learning difficulties

(MLD), severe learning difficulties (SLD) and profound and multiple learning difficulties (PMLD) can encompass a range of other factors such as physical and sensory impairments. Specific learning difficulties (SpLD) such as dyslexia, dyscalculia and dyspraxia are also included in this category as they affect one or more specific aspects of learning.

REFLECTION POINTS

■ How familiar are you with the characteristics of the different needs and disabilities present in your setting?

■ How confident are you in supporting children with these different learning needs?

■ What support do you require to be able to carry out your support role effectively?

CASE STUDY 10.1

Tom

Tom is an 8-year-old boy in the Year 4 class of a small primary school in England and he has an older sister in Year 6. Tom is very keen on football and other sports and he is sociable and popular. He has a good group of friends and he plays football with them most lunchtimes. He has a very good imagination and enjoys making up stories, although he hates writing and would much rather entertain people by acting his stories out. He has often had a leading role in assemblies and plays that the school has put on for parents. Tom is rather disorganised and tends to forget what he needs to bring school each morning.

Tom has not performed well in his end-of-year assessments, particularly in his English tests. His reading score is below that of his peers and he has underperformed in his spelling, punctuation and grammar tests. Tom has chosen a reading book that his friends have been reading even though it is too hard for him. Tom's parents are very well informed and have engaged well with the school. They are anxious to make sure everything is being done to support Tom. They are very concerned about Tom's results and believe that school is not doing enough to support Tom with his work.

REFLECTION POINTS

■ What are the key points in this scenario that suggest Tom needs some support?

■ What category of need do you think Tom comes under, according to the SEND Code of Practice 2015?

■ What support do you think Tom needs at this stage?

■ What does the school need to consider in order for Tom to respond well to the strategies it wants to implement?

Strategies to support pupils with SEND

This is not an exhaustive list of strategies and many more can be researched via the links provided at the end of the chapter. The intention here is to consider the implementation of some of these commonly used strategies and how they can have both positive and negative consequences for learners with SEND.

Provision of specialist equipment

Some children with physical difficulties will benefit from specialist equipment such as mobility aids, lifts, special chairs, table rests, pencil grips, hearing aids and communication aids, for example. These sometimes require specialist knowledge in how to use them which can raise issues for schools in terms of who should be trained to use them and what happens if the trained person is not available. The obvious answer, thinking back to the social model of disability, is for all staff to be trained. Another important consideration is the way these aids are used in the classroom. Looking back to the characteristics of inclusive practice it is important that children who benefit from the use of specialist equipment are supported and not stigmatised in any way by having to use it.

Assistive technology (explored in more depth in Chapter 7)

There has been a growth in the use of technology in schools as new applications, hardware and software are developed. Computers and tablets can provide a simple, easily accessible way for pupils to record, replay, spell-check and translate their work. This can save time and effort for pupils who have writing difficulties. Teachers can prepare resources to enable pupils to access the curriculum in ways appropriate to their needs. However is it important to consider the psychological impact of needing to use assistive technology as well as the practical aspects. Teachers who do not consider how their pupils feel when made to look different to their peers can be undermining the benefits of using technology to support pupils' learning. We can relate this to the case study above as it might be very helpful for Tom to use technology to help him spell correctly and to avoid him having to struggle with his handwriting. If he is the only child in the class using a computer then he could feel different from his friends which could have a negative effect on his confidence.

Differentiation

The SEND Code of Practice (DfE, 2015: 99) makes it clear that teachers are responsible for the progress of all the children in their class. Most children should be supported through appropriate differentiation which can be done in a number of ways, for example by scaffolding work, provision of resources, adult support or setting different tasks matched to ability. It is common practice for children to be grouped by ability in many classrooms and yet it is important to consider the effects of this. It is very likely that your role is to support lower ability groups or 'the SEN group'. The children are probably very aware of their ability in relation to others in the class, despite the attempts made to conceal this. Research has shown that ability grouping can affect children's self-esteem and motivation which can have negative effects on their confidence, attainment and progress (Marks, 2016).

Support from external agencies

To be able to support pupils with SEND effectively it may be necessary to get help from external agencies. There are many different services that might be bought in to support children, depending on their needs and difficulties. An educational psychologist will be required to assess a pupil with SEND in order to begin the process towards getting an Education, Health and Care plan. This in itself involves the agencies working together to arrive at the best possible outcomes for the child. There are often challenges for professionals from different agencies who have clearly identified roles, ways of working and areas of specialist knowledge. A conflict between agencies, a lack of communication, or differing expectations and competing priorities can all act as barriers to effective provision for children (Hodkinson, 2016).

TA support

We have explored aspects of the TA role in Chapter 1 but it is important to revisit it here. It may be your role in school, or part of it, to support a pupil or group of pupils with SEND. Many settings employ TAs for this reason, although with recent cuts to school finances this practice is undergoing change. It is thought that the deployment of TAs in this capacity stems from the Statementing process that was part of SEN provision in the previous Code of Practice of 2001. Pupils with greatest need were specified a setting and a number of hours of TA support in the Statement which was funded by the LEA. The research into TA deployment has raised questions about the value of TA support for pupils with SEND, suggesting on the one hand that there can be positives for the pupils in terms of social and emotional support and task completion (Blatchford, Russell and Webster, 2012). Negative outcomes have identified that pupils are not always challenged in their learning and some may become dependent on adult support rather than developing independent learning skills if appropriate. It has been found that TAs can sometimes act as a 'buffer' between the child and their peers which reduces their social interaction.

Working with the child/young person

This is a key principle of the SEND Code of Practice 2015. Enabling pupils with SEND to participate in the decision making about their provision is not easy but the principle behind it is widely recognised as the right of the child or young person and should be facilitated at every opportunity. Unfortunately this has not always been the case, whether intentionally or not. Care has to be taken that the situation where their views are sought is non-threatening and that the language used is accessible to the child. Children need to feel genuinely listened to and their views valued. To do this effectively for children with communication difficulties it may be necessary to use different forms of communication to enable them to participate fully. Person-centred approaches are being promoted and child-centred reviews are a way to ensure that this aspect of the SEND Code of Practice 2015 is adhered to. In this scenario the child/young person is provided with a non-threatening, supportive and positive environment in which to share their views in whatever way they are able to.

Working with the family

This is also a significant aspect of the SEND Code of Practice 2015 in which it is frequently stated that it is a requirement of schools to work with families to support children and young people with SEND. Research has shown positive relationships with parents make a significant difference to the success of SEND provision and it is important for teachers to recognise that parents have the best knowledge of their child's needs (Frederickson and Cline, 2015). This is sometimes difficult for a teacher to accept as they can feel, as the trained professional in the relationship, that their knowledge of the child is of greater importance when it comes to making decisions about the child.

There are several reasons why some families find it difficult to engage with schools and the professionals who are working with their child. We consider this in more depth in Chapter 9. Parents may have had difficult experiences of education themselves and they might have their own challenges in understanding the SEND 'system'. Lack of confidence and knowledge can make them feel vulnerable and less able to fight for their rights and those of their child. Barriers can be created if staff in schools do not recognise these issues and respond appropriately. The use of educational 'jargon' can prevent parents from feeling comfortable entering the professional world of the teacher but it is a fine line between under- and overestimating parents' understanding of the system. Staff and particularly the SENCO need good interpersonal skills to be supportive and empathic with parents, particularly when parents can feel a sense of guilt and blame when their child is first diagnosed with SEND.

REFLECTION POINTS

- How does your setting engage with parents and families of children with SEND?

- How are the children included in the decisions made about their provision?

- In the light of some of the points made about the TA role, how could the practice in your setting be adjusted?

- How would this impact on outcomes for pupils with SEND?

Chapter summary

This chapter has introduced you to different views of inclusive practice, what it means and how it can be promoted in schools. We have considered the legislative frameworks that guide how settings should provide for a range of different needs and disabilities. It is important for you as a member of staff likely to be on the front line of provision in your setting, to reflect on the effectiveness of the strategies and reasonable adjustments that are made for children and young people with SEND. This chapter has highlighted that some strategies can have very positive outcomes for pupils but if not implemented sensitively can impact negatively on children's self-esteem and social and emotional development. The challenges of providing appropriately for children with varying needs have been discussed and effective practice has been identified.

FURTHER READING

National Association for Special Educational Needs (NASEN) (2017) Available at: http://nasen.org.uk/.

Ekins, A. (2015) *The changing face of special educational needs: impact and implications for SENCOs, teachers and their schools* (2nd edn). Abingdon: Routledge.

Frederickson, N. and Cline, T. (2015) *Special educational needs, inclusion and diversity* (3rd edn). Maidenhead: Open University Press.

Following is a list of useful websites and resources to support your understanding of inclusion and different special needs and disabilities.

The Alliance for Inclusive Education – http://allfie.org.uk
British Dyslexia Association – http://bdadyslexia.org.uk/
Centre for Studies on Inclusive Education (CSIE) – http://csie.org.uk/
The Communication Trust – http://thecommunicationtrust.org.uk/
Council for Disabled Children – https://councilfordisabledchildren.org.uk/
The Disabled Children's Partnership – https://disabledchildrenspartnership.org.uk
Downs Syndrome Association – https://downs-syndrome.org.uk/
The Dyspraxia Foundation – http://dyspraxiafoundation.org.uk/
Learning Disability – http://learningdisability.co.uk/
Living with ADHD – http://livingwithadhd.co.uk/
Mencap – https://mencap.org.uk/
The National Autistic Society – http://autism.org.uk/
Scope: About Disability – https://scope.org.uk/
Sense – https://sense.org.uk/
Young Minds – https://youngminds.org.uk/

References

Ainscow, M., Dyson, A. and Booth, T. (2006) *Improving schools, developing inclusion.* London: Routledge.

Blatchford, P., Russell, A. and Webster, R. (2012) *Reassessing the impact of teaching assistants.* Abingdon: Routledge.

Booth, T. and Ainscow, M. (2011) *Index for inclusion: developing learning and participation in schools* (3rd edn). Bristol: Centre for Studies in Inclusive Education.

Department for Education (2015) *Special educational needs and disability code of practice: 0 to 25 years.* Available at: https://gov.uk/government/publications/send-code-of-practice-0-to-25 (Accessed: 12 November 2017).

Equality Act (2010) Available at: http://legislation.gov.uk/ukpga/2010/15/pdfs/ukpga_20100015_en.pdf (Accessed: 12 November 2017).

Frederickson, N. and Cline, T. (2015) *Special educational needs, inclusion and diversity* (3rd edn). Maidenhead: Open University Press.

Hodkinson, A. (2016) *Key issues in special educational needs and inclusion* (2nd edn). London: SAGE.

Marks, R. (2016) *Ability grouping in primary schools: case studies and critical debates.* Northwich: Critical Publishing.

Scope (2017) *About disability.* Available at: https://scope.org.uk/ (Accessed: 12 November 2017).

Warnock, M. (1978) *Special educational needs. Report of the Committee of Enquiry into the education of handicapped children and young people.* Cmnd. 7212 London: HMSO.

Behaviour and relationships

John Bayley

CHAPTER OVERVIEW AND AIMS

■ To reflect upon possible causes of 'difficult' behaviour

■ To consider the nature of positive relationships between practitioners and pupils

■ To consider the effectiveness of 'systems' of behaviour management

Introduction

According to the report to the House of Commons Education Committee (2011: 3), 'Good order is essential in a school if children are to be able to fulfil their learning potential.' 'Good order' is an interesting choice of phrase here; could one substitute 'positive relationships'? This chapter will have, as its main concern, ideas of how teachers' and TAs' relationships with pupils can either promote or undermine their responses to our expectations of their behaviour. In addition you will be encouraged to reflect on the effectiveness of systems of rewards and sanctions for managing pupil behaviour and we will introduce you to some alternative strategies.

Groups vulnerable to exclusion from school

The most frequent cause of exclusion from school is 'persistent disruptive behaviour' (DfE, 2017) and there are certain groups of pupils that we can identify as having much higher exclusion rates than others. Boys are three times more likely to receive both fixed-period and permanent exclusions than are girls, and the most frequent age for exclusions is Year 9 and above. Pupils entitled to free school meals were over four times more likely to be excluded, and pupils receiving SEND support were most likely of all to be excluded. The exclusion rates for looked after children are twice those of the general population. In terms of the ethnicity of excluded pupils, Black Caribbean pupils were three times more likely to be excluded, and Gypsy/Roma and Traveller children of Irish heritage had the highest rates of all (though their overall numbers are small). These figures are taken from the Department for Education's statistical reports (2017) and apply to the academic year 2015–16, though the same vulnerable groups have had very similar exclusion rates over a number of years. This is very troubling, as these pupils are not only excluded from school, but also have a higher risk of eventually being unemployed, or becoming part of the criminal justice system.

REFLECTION POINTS

- Take one of the vulnerable groups listed above that you support in school. Why do you think this group is at risk of exclusion from school?

- Locate any government guidance that is in place to support this group – how effective do you think it is?

- What support is in place in your school for this group?

- What kinds of support do you give, and how effective do you think it is?

Possible causes of difficult behaviour

It is all too easy for professionals to simply dismiss children's behaviour as 'naughty', 'difficult', or 'challenging'. These are the presenting behaviours, but we need to remember that there will always be underlying causes, which often we will have no access to. These may range from children's temperaments, family factors, peer relationships, cultural and media influences, genetic or neurobiological reasons (Atkinson and Hornby, 2002). Of course, conditions that are 'categorised' as Special Educational Needs and Disabilities under the SEND Code of Practice 2014, for example autism, ADHD and mental health difficulties, may equally impact on pupils' behaviour. All this is complex, but whatever the possible cause of 'difficult' behaviour in a child, professionals need to display empathy. It can be extremely difficult for a teacher or TA to remain objective in the face of challenges from pupils, which may, on occasion, feel personal, but it helps to remember that these are children and young people who are vulnerable, even though this may not necessarily be apparent. It is wise to be calm in difficult situations; of course education professionals are human, and, therefore prone to anger when provoked, but there are ways of remaining objective even when you are not necessarily calm – this will be discussed later in this chapter.

REFLECTION POINTS

- Think of a child that you know who displays 'difficult' behaviour.

- What do you know of her/his personal circumstances?

- Carefully observe her/him in the context of a lesson. Can you identify any 'trigger points' for particular behaviours?

- Are there any ways in which these could be minimised or avoided?

- Carefully observe the same child in the playground. What, if any, are the differences in behaviour? Reflect upon why this might be.

Behaviour and learning

It is worth emphasising from the beginning that the management of behaviour cannot be separated from the management of learning; put simply, if children are motivated and engaged by the tasks they are asked to complete, they are more likely to behave positively.

Motivation to learn is a key factor. Intrinsic motivation – interest in the task for its own sake – is, arguably, more powerful that extrinsic motivation – performing for rewards, or to avoid sanctions. For example, a child may become absorbed in a specific history project that has been well prepared by the teacher. Often, children are most motivated when the topic is perceived as relevant and purposeful; a topic on the local area might fall into this category. However, even if the topic itself may not be of intrinsic interest to the child, if teachers and TAs can find ways of making the tasks motivating – active, well-modelled, carefully sequenced – broken down into small steps if necessary – children may well become motivated. Best of all is if we can use the child's own interests as a vehicle for learning. Giving choices about *how* pupils tackle the task, which gives children some ownership of their learning behaviour (Ellis and Tod, 2015), may be helpful in motivating pupils.

Perceived success is another key factor in motivating pupils. Tasks should be set at an appropriate level – sufficiently challenging (within what Vygotsky termed the 'zone of proximal development') so that the child can complete them with some success. Using a range of paired and collaborative tasks will be helpful here. This will raise the levels of self-esteem, as the child will perceive that s/he is a successful learner, and will gain the teacher's approbation, which could be in the form of targeted praise. Strategies such as sharing the work with others, presenting or displaying the work, etc. may contribute to what Haydn, (2012: 62) identifies as the 'pure' path to pupil engagement, in that the child will become prepared to accept difficulty, learn from mistakes and celebrate achievement.

CASE STUDY 11.1

Michael

Michael was a Year 6 pupil, who struggled with reading and writing, and was therefore difficult to motivate, which resulted in frequent refusal to work, and other low-level unco-operative behaviour. One Monday morning, when Michael arrived in class, his teacher asked him if he had had a good weekend. Michael replied that he had been fishing with his Dad, and proceeded to relate, with great enthusiasm, details of this activity; he was clearly very knowledgeable about this topic, so the teacher suggested that he might produce a booklet about it to go into the class library (this was something that many of the other children had previously undertaken). With support for spelling etc., and with plenty of time and encouragement, Michael did, indeed, produce a very interesting booklet to share with his peers, but the effects were more wide-ranging, in that his writing and reading began to improve, and so did his behaviour in class. It was as if, by chance, the teacher had found the 'key' to unlock Michael's motivation.

REFLECTION POINTS

- Think of examples that you have observed where children have been motivated in the task for its own sake.

- Reflect upon possible reasons for this – what was it about the task that brought this about?

- What did the teacher or TA do to encourage this?

- What changes in behaviour did you observe as a result?

Relationships with pupils

Research has demonstrated that pupil-teacher relationships shape children's attitudes to school, and therefore, to attitudes and behaviour (Haydn, 2012; Riley and Rustique-Forrester, 2002). Thus we have a body of evidence that identifies what pupils (especially those who are at risk of disaffection, and possible exclusion as identified earlier in the chapter) will respond to positively. Some of these teacher characteristics may appear to be obvious, but they are, nevertheless, key to gaining pupils' positive engagement. They include:

- Being 'human' – treating pupils as individuals with their own likes and dislikes, interests and abilities. In the case study of Michael it is clear to see that his teacher is interested in Michael 'as a person'. Rooney (in Farrell and Ainscow, 2002: 96) identifies this as 'problem-free talk', where teachers demonstrate that they are interested in the child as more than the sum of their behaviour. Listening to their concerns and having a sense of humour, which can be employed to minimise potential conflict and confrontation, are also perceived as positive teacher characteristics.

- Being helpful and supportive to pupils, knowing their needs and supporting them. This includes taking time to explain tasks clearly, and to explain the task again to an individual if necessary.

- Being in control of the class. Pupils do not respect teachers who cannot, or do not, have rules that all can subscribe to.

- Using a variety of teaching styles. Pupils dislike teachers who have a non-changing teaching routine (see discussion of motivation, above).

- Fairness. Pupils expect teachers, and other adults, to be fair, and to treat all pupils equally – for example, children dislike the whole class being kept in because of one pupil's (or a group of pupils') misdemeanour.

- Willingness to reward pupils for making good progress, not just for high attainment.

These are only some of the teacher characteristics that pupils perceive as positive; if teachers (and others) are to become skilled at managing behaviour, they will need to consider how they are behaving in these areas.

CASE STUDY 11.2

Marshal

Marshal, a Year 10 pupil, was given some mathematics homework on a new topic concerning problems with percentages, without the teacher explaining how to complete them. Instead he was asked to access an online tutorial and then complete the examples. He did not understand this tutorial, even though he watched it twice, so got most of the examples wrong. His teacher, upon marking this homework, told him that he would have to complete them again, this time in detention. Only when Marshal protested that his grandfather, who is a university lecturer, had also not understood the tutorial, did the teacher relent. Nevertheless, she did not further explain how to go about completing these mathematical problems.

- How might the teacher have interacted more effectively with Marshal to support both his learning and his self-esteem?

- What could the effects be on Marshal's behaviour if the teacher continues to penalise him for not understanding his work?

ACTIVITY

Reflect upon your own interactions with children.

- How might you further develop these?

Strategies for behaviour management in the classroom

In this section, we will consider the use of rewards and sanctions, managing more challenging pupils in the classroom, and conflict resolution.

Rewards

Schools commonly have behaviour management policies which include the giving of rewards, usually taking the form of merit points, sticker charts, stars, online icons etc. Frequently, these may accumulate so that 'star' pupils receive small rewards. In some classrooms merit charts are publicly displayed, which may well serve to encourage many of the children, but may discourage those whose behaviour mitigates against the gaining of rewards – a very public failure, which may cause some of them to become increasingly disaffected at school. Equally, some schools have assemblies where they praise children whose behaviour has improved, but we need to bear in mind that, for some of those children, this is too public an arena – they would prefer such praise to be more discreet.

The use of rewards is, of course, based on behaviourist theory, and there is a considerable body of criticism of such methods as inhibiting and interrupting students' absorption in their activities (Porter, 2000). Equally, it may reduce the intrinsic motivation and the enthusiasm for learning, and risks children becoming dependent on a reward for their actions.

Sanctions

Again, schools frequently use a range of sanctions to control pupils' behaviour, which typically may include loss of break times, detention, or missing 'golden time'. It is worth teachers, and other adults, asking themselves whether it is generally the same pupils on the receiving end of sanctions – if so we may need to consider whether they are working. The danger is that such pupils may become increasingly disaffected with all aspects of school life, and may even take a perverse pleasure in misbehaving, especially if it gives them the attention that they may crave. We might argue that, in general, sanctions probably work best with those who do not really need them.

The power of behaviour agreements

There will always be children for whom the usual range of rewards and sanctions will not be effective. Here, the use of agreements, which set targets for behaviour, can be very powerful. Rooney, in Farrell and Ainscow (2002: 88–99) discusses these issues in an interesting and detailed way. It works something like this:

When the child is calm (in other words, when the difficult behaviour is not happening), ask him/her to reflect upon the behaviour ('How do you feel about. . . .'). This immediately hands some power to the pupil, and can be the beginning of a dialogue. Ask the pupil what he/she thinks they can do about it ('How would you like your behaviour to be?'). Ask how you can support this. What you have done is place responsibility on the pupil, without being confrontational – you have not directly made negative comments about the behaviour, and you have asked open, non-threatening questions. This might be turned into a more formalised set of specific behavioural targets, with the agreement of the pupil, whom you have empowered. This could be in the form of a (private) chart, with a space for each lesson for the week, with very specific targets – e.g. 'I will work without disturbing others in the class'. It is better not to have too many targets (indeed, one target may well be sufficient to begin with) and it is helpful to involve the pupil in assessing whether the target has been met, lesson by lesson, as, again, this gives more ownership to him/her.

REFLECTION POINTS

▪ Can you think of a pupil who might benefit from a target-setting approach?

▪ Can you formulate some open questions that you might ask?

▪ How might the agreement read, in a more formalised way?

Management of the classroom

Much has been written about how to manage (rather than *control*) classrooms – see especially any of the texts by Bill Rogers. Some of the most useful ideas are summarised here:

▪ If classroom rules are phrased positively, and are *genuinely* the result of dialogue between teacher and pupils, children are more likely to feel that they have some ownership – they are *their* rules.

▪ Have a plan for the movement of children in transitional phases of the lesson – give very clear instructions.

▪ Keep the emotional temperature of the classroom low; use the minimum means necessary to manage behaviour. A look at an 'offender' may be sufficient, or a gesture. If not, use proximity (move closer to the child(ren)'s space. Pause and wait – but not for very long. Or you may decide to 'tactically ignore', to use Rogers' phrase, and deal with it later.

▪ Do not over-react; defuse potential confrontations, maybe with humour, or the use of a simple directional comment.

▪ Be very clear about your behaviour expectations – avoid using vague phrases. For example, say: 'I would like you all to look at me and listen carefully', rather than 'Is everybody ready?'.

▪ Give clear choices with pupils whose behaviour is interfering with learning – e.g. 'You need to complete this by the end of the lesson, or you will need to do it at break time'. This, of course, assumes that you have checked that the child understands the task.

CASE STUDY 11.3

James

James was a teaching assistant asked to cover a lesson with a 'challenging' Year 6 class during the teacher's absence. Whilst the children were working on the task that had been set, Sean got up from his seat and began shuffling through some papers on a table – he was not disturbing other pupils. The TA went over to Sean and yelled at him to 'sit down', which was met by an absolute refusal. He then repeated, even more loudly 'Sit down!' Finally James, increasing the already high volume, shouted 'I'll count to five', and proceeded to do so – Sean remained where he was. The TA, defeated, walked away. This confrontation was enjoyed by the whole class, who then proved difficult for the TA to settle back to being on task.

- What were the problems with this approach?

- How might James have minimised his response to this incident to avoid confrontation?

Chapter summary

This chapter has identified that there are a number of principles of behaviour management, both explicit and implicit. We have recognised that most important of all is the power of effective pupil-teacher relationships and the benefits of 'being human'. Although systems of rewards and sanctions are commonly in place in schools, approaches to managing behaviour that involve mutual respect, dialogue in many forms, the giving of responsibility and ownership at an appropriate level are more likely to support and sustain the teacher-pupil relationship.

FURTHER READING

Adams, K. (2009) *Behaviour for learning in the primary school.* Exeter: Learning Matters.

Lever, C. (2011) *Understanding challenging behaviour in inclusive classrooms.* Harlow: Pearson Education.

Roffey, S. (2011) *Challenging behaviour in schools.* London: Sage.

Rogers, B. (2015) *Classroom behaviour.* London: Sage.

Vizard, D. (2009) *Meeting the needs of disaffected students.* London: Continuum.

References

Atkinson, M. and Hornby, G. (2002) *Mental health handbook for schools*. London: Routledge.

Department for Education (DfE) (2014) *Special educational needs and disability code of practice: 0 to 25 years*. Available at: https://gov.uk/government/publications/send-code-of-practice-0-to-25 (Accessed: 12 November 2017).

Department for Education (DfE) (2017) *Outcomes for children looked after by local authorities in England, 31st March, 2016*. Available at: https://gov.uk/government/uploads/system/uploads/attachment_data/file/602087/SFR12_2017_Text.pdf (Accessed: 13 November 2017).

Department for Education (DfE) (2017) *Fixed period and permanent exclusions in England: 2015–2016*. Available at: https://gov.uk/government/uploads/system/uploads/attachment_data/file/645075/SFR35_2017_text.pdf (Accessed: 13 November 2017).

Ellis, S. and Tod, J. (2015) *Promoting behaviour for learning in the classroom*. Abingdon: Routledge.

Farrell, P. and Ainscow, M. (2002) *Making special education inclusive*. London: David Fulton.

Haydn, T. (2012) *Managing pupil behaviour*. Abingdon: Routledge.

House of Commons Education Committee (2011) *Behaviour and discipline in schools*. London: The Stationery Office Ltd.

Porter, L. (2000) *Behaviour in schools*. Buckingham: Open University Press.

Riley, K. and Rustique-Forrester, E. (2002) *Working with disaffected students*. London: Paul Chapmen Publishing.

Vygotsky, L. (1962) *Thought and language*. Cambridge, MA: MIT Press.

Inclusion, diversity and English as an additional language (EAL)

Chris Watts and Parminder Assi

CHAPTER OVERVIEW AND AIMS

- To gain an appreciation of linguistic diversity

- To gain an understanding of how language is part of learner identity

- To review strategies to support pupils using EAL

- To reflect on your personal experiences of language and consider how these inform your work with pupils using EAL

Introduction

For many of you it will be your role to support learners with special or additional educational needs, to give literacy support, general classroom support and also to work with pupils learning English as an Additional Language (EAL). Some schools will have specialist EAL teachers or bilingual TAs, but it is an ever-increasing area of responsibility for all TAs. This chapter aims to provide you with the information you need to support pupils using EAL effectively and sensitively. You will gain an understanding of linguistic diversity and what EAL means. You will be introduced to concepts and a range of strategies that will support your teaching of children using EAL.

What has diversity to do with EAL?

In 2016, there were over 1 million children thought to be using English as an additional language in English schools, 20.1% of children in primary schools and

15.7% of children in secondary schools (DfE, 2016). These children's families and their roots come from an ever-increasing number of countries across the world; this increasing diversity is a result of globalisation and a wide range of issues including economic development, climate change, international instability and breaking down of barriers by communication and transportation.

There are six languages originating in the four countries that make up the UK. These are: English, Welsh, Cornish, Gaelic, Irish and Scots. There are also numerous other languages spoken in the UK: Polish, Punjabi, Urdu, Bengali, Gujarati, Arabic, French, Portuguese, Spanish and Tamil are each spoken by over 100,000 people.

Schools are required to promote and instil British values, tolerance of all religions, respect for all and for the rule of law. The emphasis on equality of opportunity applies to all children in our schools. Some of the most disadvantaged children are also fleeing from armed conflicts or persecution, and are refugees or asylum seekers. These children face new challenges along with learning a new language and negotiating different educational and cultural expectations. Some children have been left without school places for long periods of time. The school may be one of the few supportive environments children encounter and the TA can play a key role in their inclusion into school and society. A whole school commitment to inclusion and race equality with the involvement of school leadership, teachers, teaching assistants and all other adults in school is key to setting up a holistic experience for these children.

REFLECTION POINTS

■ Imagine your own teenage self or a young relative of yours, being forced out of your home and sent to live by yourself in a non-English speaking country.

■ How would you cope?

■ How would you feel?

■ What would you need to support you in the early stages?

Learning a new language

First of all EAL is not a disease, so where you may hear staff in school talking about students with severe EAL, do not be afraid. These pupils have the ability to live in and use a language other than English, and they will learn to live in and use English naturally, quite often in a short period of time. For many of us, this is a skill we will never master as we only speak English, and may have struggled with learning French or German at school. We may still not be able to have a basic conversation in it. For some of us, however, being able to speak two languages (bilingual), or more (multilingual) enables us to have different ways of expressing ourselves and different ways of looking at the world. The words we use are the building blocks of our thinking. For example, in Hindi there is no specific word for cousin; cousins are colloquially *paji*, i.e. brother, or *pahunji*, sister. The relationships between cousins become more like siblings. The way we put words together to make phrases and sentences affects the way we see the world. Children who are developing this ability will be a vital bridge to the wider world for all of us in the UK.

Our job in school is to enable pupils using EAL to have full access to the whole curriculum as quickly and securely as possible. For pupils who are new to English, at whatever age, there will be a process of developing basic survival English, which Cummins (2000) calls Basic Interpersonal Communicative Skills (BICS). The ability of children to develop and negotiate the playground and school environment will develop relatively naturally, but in order to succeed in school they need to develop Cognitive Academic Language Proficiency (CALP) (Cummins, 2000). Cognitive Academic language is not what we normally use with friends or when sending text messages, but we use it in more formal situations such as writing up a science experiment or writing an essay. This is language for thinking, reasoning, decision making, problem solving, and the understanding of knowledge. Cummins suggests that it takes learners, on average, two years to achieve a functional, social use of a second language, or BICS, but that it usually takes between five and seven years (sometimes longer) for some bilingual learners to achieve a level of academic linguistic proficiency or CALP, comparable to their monolingual English-speaking peers.

Almost all schools in the UK have pupils who speak, use and live in two or more languages. This ranges from pupils who may be bilingual and completely at ease speaking, reading and writing in two languages, such as English and Welsh, or English and Urdu. There are also pupils who are beginning the process of becoming bilingual, who have little or no use of English. The term EAL also includes children who speak English as their main language but who come from a family that uses another language in their daily life. There is a wide range of experiences among school pupils, so we must be careful of labelling, stigmatising, and stereotyping children identified in school as using EAL. It is important to remember that EAL is a process, children do not 'have' EAL, they 'use' EAL. EAL is not a special educational need; children using EAL can be gifted and talented but may not be able to express their talents in English.

Pellegrino (2005) writes that when learners are placed in a second language environment there can be threats to a learner's self-image. If you lose the ability to communicate your feelings and thoughts, if you cannot joke, then you can lose a sense of self. Language and literacy develop through the context of the home and community. Bilingual children have at least two contexts for making meaning about language and literacy. The best approach to ensure children develop positive self-image is to acknowledge all the languages that they speak. Indeed, development of literacy and language in a first, or home, language supports the development of English; see Cummins' iceberg model (1991).

Look at the following table showing a group of children in one English classroom, who all identify as Urdu speakers, and we see a complex picture of the use of languages in one class. Each child is uniquely engaged with the world with complex social and communicative interactions in at least two languages, and if we reduce these complexities to 'an EAL child', 'an EAL learner', or 'a pupil with EAL', we deny the richness of their experiences and skills, and limit their potential.

Table 12.1 Children in one class identified as EAL learners who speak Urdu

Children in one class identified as EAL learners who speak Urdu			
Child	First language spoken	Second language spoken	Third language spoken
Ahmed	Urdu; speaks to mum and grandma. Child prefers Urdu as the others do not understand English	English; siblings and cousins	
Ayesha	English; prefers English as this is the language she uses more	Urdu; is literate and speaks language. Speaks language to mum, grandma and granddad	Spanish; learning in school
Salma	English	Urdu; speaks to mum, family members	Arabic; learns to read in mosque but cannot understand or write it
Mariam	English; is literate, prefers language as she is more confident in using this language	Panjabi; speaks to family members, can write a little	Urdu; speaks a little to extended family members
Nadim	English; speaks with siblings	Urdu; speaks to mum and dad, has learned a little, taught by mum	Russian; younger sibling learns from interactive tool and teaches older brother
Fatima	English; speaks with mum and siblings	Urdu; extended family members, older sister teaches younger siblings the language, reading and speaking	

REFLECTION POINTS

■ What are the implications for schools knowing that it can take seven years for children to achieve CALP?

■ How would you think these children using EAL would feel starting to learn German from scratch?

■ Would they be more or less comfortable than a monolingual (English only) child?

ACTIVITY

■ Watch part of a Modern Foreign Language class, perhaps French or Spanish, and observe how monolingual pupils compare to multilingual pupils in learning a new language.

CASE STUDY 12.1

Bilingual TAs

Here are some comments from TAs educated in English schools, talking about their feelings about learning languages:

As a bilingual myself, I felt that throughout my own schooling I never felt that this was a gift or 'something special'; rather, it was a part of my identity which although unintentionally, I would have concealed due to the little importance placed on being able to speak more than one language…

I know I don't know any languages, and I'm either not worried or I am ashamed… I can only guess at what circumstances children learn English. I gave up on languages… I have to do better than how I was taught languages.

I never learned to speak another language in addition to English. I often question if this has been down to ignorance and automatically assuming that I would never need to speak another language. Perhaps I thought I would never need to. However, it dawns upon me as I get older that I was naïve to think that I would never need to learn another language.

I lived and worked in China and while I was able to pick up some basic phrases and key vocabulary, I never got anywhere close to mastering what is quite a complex language…the limitations of being denied full expression of my thoughts, feelings and opinions could be incredibly frustrating as it effectively meant that large chunks of my character were 'lost'.

By reflecting on our own relationship with language it is possible to see how our identity and our view of what goes on in school is formed. This will help us to empathise with children using EAL.

ACTIVITY

Talk to some bilingual pupils in school about their feelings and relationships with the languages they use. These are some questions you may want to ask:

- Do you like speaking two languages?

- What languages are you fluent in and how did you learn them?

- In what situations do you use each of these languages and what impact has it had on your life?

- How could you use your bilingual talent in your future?

- Do you feel that English and an English identity are given priority over your home language?

When you have done this think about what you have learned from these pupils and how you might want to approach working with them in the future.

Who are our pupils using English as an Additional Language?

The DfES (2004) definition of English as an Additional Language has the following categories. These are not in any order of significance and there are overlaps between them.

- Learners whose parents are working and studying and are in England for short periods of time; this might include children of casual workers, and children of university lecturers

- Learners who are second and third generation members of settled communities

- Learners who are children of recent or new migrants from Europe or wider afield

- 'Isolated learners' who are in school settings that have little prior experience of bilingual pupils. You may be working in a rural school which has a very small number of children using EAL, but their need for support may be more explicit than in a school which has significant experience and resources to support EAL

■ Learners who are recent arrivals and new to English, with little or no experience of schooling

■ Learners who are recent arrivals and new to English, but who are already literate in their first language

■ Learners whose education has been disrupted because of war and other traumatic experiences. The families may be classified as refugees or asylum seekers. Some of these children have not attended school or have been out of education for a period of time. They may have experienced unstable social situations and have high levels of anxiety or emotional distress, so it is important that school provides a safe and supportive environment with quiet spaces when they can go to reflect, pray or rest

TA support for EAL learners

TAs support pupils using EAL in three ways:

■ helping to identify the needs of EAL learners and facilitating their integration into school

■ supporting and assessing EAL learners within the classroom

■ supporting the needs of EAL learners outside the classroom and throughout school.

We will now look at each of these in detail.

Identifying the needs of EAL learners and facilitating their integration into school

Your role as TA can include being involved in the admission of new arrivals, participating in dialogue with children and parents, formal collection of background information, and observing EAL learners, to feed into mainstream teachers' assessment and planning.

One of the key steps for schools is to identify how much English a pupil knows and can use. The DfE (2016) requirements for the twice-yearly school census use the following five codes to assess EAL pupils:

Practice varies from school to school in who carries out this assessment. Some schools have teachers with specialist qualifications in EAL who are trained in assessment; other schools use administrative staff. TAs are called to do this work in some schools. There are no generic assessment tools, but there are various

Table 12.2 Five codes to assess EAL pupils

A. New to English	May use first language for learning and other purposes. May remain completely silent in the classroom. May be copying/repeating some words or phrases.
B. Early acquisition	May follow day-to-day social communication in English and participate in learning activities with support. Beginning to use spoken English for social purposes.
C. Developing competence	May participate in learning activities with increasing independence. Able to express self orally in English, but structural inaccuracies are still apparent.
D. Competent	Oral English will be developing well, enabling successful engagement in activities across the curriculum. Can read and understand a wide variety of texts. Written English may lack complexity and contain occasional evidence of errors in structure.
E. Fluent	Can operate across the curriculum to a level of competence equivalent to that of a pupil who uses English as his/her first language.
N. Not yet assessed	This is used when the school has not yet had time to assess the pupil's proficiency.

procedures available (see NASSEA, NALDIC etc). Whoever does this work will need additional training and support.

The school you are working in and the class you are supporting may also have different and contradictory views about the role of English and home languages in learning compared to other classes and other schools. Some teachers argue that only English should be spoken in the classroom in England. Others argue that a multilingual classroom is not only beneficial to EAL students but to non-EAL students.

REFLECTION POINT

Surely children born here should be speaking English when they come to school?

The children are noisy and silly when I ask them to use their first language – how do I know that they are on task?

■ What do you think of these TA comments?

ACTIVITY

Talk with the EAL co-ordinator in the school.

■ What are their views on the use of home language in the classroom?

■ Who do you – and they – think should be doing the assessment of EAL learners?

■ What do you think about the withdrawal of children from the classroom for specific language support versus immersion in the class?

Supporting EAL learners within the classroom

Supporting whole class teaching

Working in class in collaboration with the class teacher is a vital part of the TAs role. This can include:

- finding appropriate visuals in advance to help EAL learners access the lesson

- role-playing with the class or subject teacher to show what the expectations of a task are – e.g. demonstrating and modelling the expected language for group discussion ('What do you think?' ' I don't really agree with that because ...')

- facilitating group work in class – not necessarily the same group each time, and this can be groups that include pupils using English fluently in a range of situations and subjects

- pre-teaching key vocabulary before a topic is tackled in class

- giving beginner EAL learners an opportunity to rehearse an answer to a question privately before speaking in front of the class

- buddying up, i.e. pairing learners who share a first language so they can discuss a topic in more depth, using talk partners and paired reading schemes

- supporting EAL learners' effective use of bilingual dictionaries and/or translation software such as wordreference.com

Using a bilingual dictionary is fairly straightforward, but using translation software can be problematic. Some languages used by children in school are difficult to translate with software. For example 'hello' translates into Tigrinyan, the Eritrean language, as ሰላም. How can you read this or pronounce it? Get your pupils using EAL to teach you and others in the class some of their first language, such as basic greetings. See the Newbury school 'language of the month' website for wonderful examples of bilingual children using their expertise to teach.

Small group or one-to-one work

Working in small groups can better offer pupils the opportunities of peer teaching, group investigation and project work with an emphasis on co-operation in learning, which is important for pupils' socio-cultural development. Small groups or individual teaching can also offer the chance for one-to-one exchanges with a TA. However, there are issues surrounding the management of such group and individual sessions, especially those that take place outside the classroom, the stigma of withdrawal, as well as the potential for falling behind in the curriculum due to the constraints of withdrawal classes. We discuss this issue for children with SEND in Chapter 10.

Talking with English language learners

There are some key principles involved in talking with pupils learning EAL.

First of all, give time and space. Beginners require a 'receptive' period when they will be listening and taking in information but not necessarily engaging in the learning. Listening constantly and trying to make sense of each word and phrase is very tiring.

Next, listen carefully, and re-cast what children say. Look at the exchanges below.

Teacher 1: What's the capital of England?
Pupil: I thinking London
Teacher 1: Good, next question

This first example is a typical display question, which is concerned with getting what the teacher knows is the correct display of knowledge from the pupil, but doesn't help develop their usage of correct grammatical structures.

Teacher 2: What's the capital of England?
Pupil: I thinking London
Teacher 2: Wrong, you say 'I think it's London'

This is better, giving the correct structure, but the pupil's answer isn't wrong, it just has a poor structure, and could leave the pupil thinking they have failed.

Teacher 3: What's the capital of England?
Pupil: I thinking London
Teacher 3: Yes that's good, I think it's London; now you say, 'I think it's London'
Pupil: I think it's London
Teacher 3: Yes, good. Now, why do you think it's London?

This teacher's questioning and response is better, supporting the pupil's language development and also encouraging deeper thought and giving opportunities to extend language skills.

Interactions between pupils and teachers or TAs can follow a common pattern involving three moves: initiation (usually a teacher's question where they already know the answer), a response by the pupil, and some teacher feedback, which is often evaluative in nature. The feedback often evaluates the pupil's response briefly and then the adult moves to another pupil with another question. However, it is crucial for the teacher to extend the pupil further. TAs need to approach questioning with the aim of stretching the pupil cognitively and linguistically by avoiding a simple immediate evaluation. It is also important not to jump into activities with questioning. Take care to personalise the topic of the session with. non-task-related introductions, and by settling the pupil into the activity, before asking questions to scaffold learning, not just following the three-step initiation/ response/feedback questioning process; see Wardman (2013).

Asking questions to extend children's ideas

Murphy (2014) shows that children using and learning EAL had lower English vocabularies than monolingual English speakers. She states that 'vocabulary knowledge and expressive vocabulary in particular, is a powerful discriminator' and we should, therefore 'actively teach vocabulary to enable all students to build their vocabulary breadth and depth.'

Vocabulary breadth is to know the meanings of many words, including multiple words for the same, or related, concepts. For example we can describe what we do with our dinner as: eat, munch, scoff, gobble, devour, consume, ingest – depending on who we are talking to and how we are feeling.

Depth is to know multiple meanings, both common and uncommon, for a given word. Learners of EAL may find it hard to attach more than a single meaning to each word e.g. the word 'solution' has different meanings in maths, chemistry and history. If your understanding of the word 'cycle' only relates to a bicycle, the concept of a water cycle is completely different.

Deepening vocabulary: think of synonyms and antonyms for words – hot becomes: boiling, warm, humid, stifling, burning… and then cold. Think of the continuum: cold, cool, tepid, warm, hot.

Teacher 3:   What do you know about London?
Pupil: I thinking London is… is big city.
Teacher 3:   Yes that's good, it is a big city. Tell me more… can you think of other words to describe a big city?

Specific strategies for more advanced EAL learners

As we have already seen, pupils using EAL may take between five and seven years to reach Cognitive Academic Language Proficiency. We therefore need to continue to support more advanced EAL learners to achieve their full potential.

Plan speaking and listening activities

- Value and use the first language
- Share and practise new ideas

- Provide good models of English

- Focus on subject-specific language

- Reinforce key vocabulary

Encouragement to write at length

- Aspects of writing need long-term development – from Key Stage 1 or 2 onwards:

- Brainstorming and mind-mapping around key words

- Using personal experience to add to content

- Writing regularly at length, with support, for example guided writing

- Extensive reading to become familiar with styles and genres

- Encouragement and support to try more ambitious phrases, sentences and texts

- Strengthening the ability to imagine

Supporting the needs of EAL learners outside the classroom

School is a site where pupils not only work with their classmates, the teachers, and the TAs, but interact and learn with others from the wider school and community. You have a role in promoting inclusion across the school. You may be involved in working with a range of people to provide a rich environment for pupils to develop their English skills to access and engage with the whole of the school curriculum. To help pupils using EAL, TAs work with older pupils, other members of staff such as bilingual non-teaching staff, and community volunteers, where they may be engaged in a range of activities from shared reading and discussions to social and cultural activities. You may also be working in partnership with parents and carers to maintain regular positive contact and to inform about individual targets and progress, to help inform about the British education system including how teachers teach and how children are assessed, to encourage maintenance of the first language, and support family literacy activity in English and in the first or home language.

What if I am bilingual or multilingual myself?

Bilingual teaching assistants can:

- contribute to school awareness of the needs of bilingual learners

- facilitate appropriate use of EAL learners' other language skills

- interpret key words and instructions

- use their first language to explore concepts in greater depth

- feed knowledge of learners' understanding of key concepts into the teacher's assessment and planning

- facilitate liaison with parents.

REFLECTION POINT

Think how parents/carers can help with their children's learning at school and home.

- What other personal qualities, experiences and skills do you have that will specifically help EAL pupils?

ACTIVITY

Talk to parents of EAL children about their hopes and concerns.

- What do they want from school? What do the parents teach their children at home?

Chapter summary

As we have seen, our children in our schools have multiple identities, speak multiple languages and engage in mixed cultural activities; they have local, regional, national and transnational affiliations. Often these differences are not seen as positives. However, we must allow children a place to explore differences, and to challenge assumptions. We need to give voice to each uniquely individual child and value what they bring to school. We must harness differences and allow their peers to explore and question the world they live in, to strengthen our schools and support community cohesion.

The content we have covered in this chapter will be helpful for all of the pupils in your class and their diverse backgrounds, experiences, and identities. We hope that this knowledge will improve your engagement with your local community, your experiences of talking and sharing information with parents/carers and your support for your own children and their language needs and difficulties.

FURTHER READING

British Council (2017) *Refugees and asylum seekers.* Available at: https://eal.britishcouncil.org/teachers/refugees-and-asylum-seekers (Accessed: 20 September 2017).

British Council (2017) *Countries, cultures, languages and education systems.* Available at: https://eal.britishcouncil.org/teachers/countries-cultures-languages-and-education-systems (Accessed: 20 September 2017).

Department for Children, Schools and Families (DCSF) (2007) *New arrivals excellence programme: guidance and resources for meeting the needs of new arrivals in primary and secondary schools.* London: DCSF Publications. Available at: https://eal.britishcouncil.org/sites/default/files/document-files/New%20Arrivals%20Guidance.pdf (Accessed: 15 March 2018).

National Association for Language Development in the Curriculum (2017) *Welcome, admission, induction and peer support.* Available at: https://naldic.org.uk/eal-teaching-and-learning/outline-guidance/ealrefugee/refwel/ (Accessed: 30 October 2017).

The UN Refugee Agency (2017) *The world in numbers.* Available at: http://popstats.unhcr.org/en/overview (Accessed: 20 September 2017).

References

Cummins, J. (1991) 'Language development and academic learning', in L. Malave and G. Duquette (eds), *Language, culture and cognition.* Clevedon: Multilingual Matters.

Cummins, J. (2000) *Language, power and pedagogy: bilingual children in the crossfire.* Clevedon: Multilingual Matters.

Department for Children, Schools and Families (DCSF) (2007) *New arrivals excellence programme: guidance and resources for meeting the needs of new arrivals in primary and secondary schools.* Available at: https://eal.britishcouncil.org/sites/default/files/document-files/New%20Arrivals%20Guidance.pdf (Accessed: 30 October 2017).

Department for Education and Skills (DfES) (2004) *Aiming high: a guide to good practice – supporting the education of asylum seeking and refugee children.* Available at: http://webarchive.nationalarchives.gov.uk/20120106191112/https://education.gov.uk/publications/eOrderingDownload/DfES-0287-2004.pdf (Accessed: 30 October 2017).

Department for Education (DfE) (2016) *Schools, pupils and their characteristics: January 2016,* SFR20/2016. Available at: https://gov.uk/government/uploads/system/uploads/attachment_data/file/552342/SFR20_2016_Main_Text.pdf (Accessed: 12 November 2017).

Murphy, V. (2014) *A systematic review of intervention research examining English language and literacy development in children with English as an additional language (EAL).* Oxford: The Bell Foundation.

National Association for Language Development in the Curriculum (NALDIC) (2017) *Welcome, admission, induction and peer support.* Available at: https://naldic.org.uk/eal-teaching-and-learning/outline-guidance/ealrefugee/refwel/ (Accessed: 30 October 2017).

Pellegrino, V.A. (2005) *Study abroad and second language use: constructing the self.* Cambridge: Cambridge University Press.

Wardman, C. (2013) 'Interactions between EAL pupils, specialist teachers and TAs during withdrawal from the mainstream in UK primary schools'. *Education 3–13.* Vol. 41, No. 6, pp 647–663.

PART IV
Professional development

Undertaking a small-scale research project

Allison Tatton

CHAPTER OVERVIEW AND AIMS

This chapter aims to encourage you to think about:

- the sort of project you might want to undertake in your school/setting

- the type of project it is realistic to carry out

- some of the challenges and benefits of undertaking a research project and how it can be advantageous to your role in your setting

- how you might go about enlisting the support of others.

Introduction

Towards the end of their Foundation Degree students are often required to undertake a research project. They often feel anxious about doing this and you may be no different. However, undertaking a research project allows you to bring together many of the skills you have developed throughout your degree and relate this to your workplace. Some of the skills you use will include academic writing, critical reading, analysis, reflection, synthesis of information, sourcing of appropriate literature, negotiation, organisation and time management (see Chapter 3 for more about some of these).

Before you undertake any research, you will almost certainly need to undertake some research training. This chapter is not about how to undertake research or the benefit of employing one type of approach or data collection method over another. There are many excellent books on the market that will help you to do that (some of these are listed in the 'Further reading' section at the end of this chapter). This chapter will help you to think about: what type of project you want to undertake; what type of project it is realistic to undertake in your setting/school; how to design a project that is 'doable'; how you might want to go about negotiating your project; getting other colleagues in school on board; factors to consider when carrying out your project; undertaking your project and writing it up. It will also help you to think about how the project could be useful to the school/setting you are working in and how it can help benefit your career, especially if you are looking to continue with your studies.

Choosing a topic to study

Some students come to their research project with a clear understanding of the topic they want to research and the research questions they want to address, but these students are usually in a minority. More often students will arrive at this point in their study with some ideas but with little focus. However, because of the pressure to get started this can cause a great deal of anxiety and even stress.

Your research project is likely to be the longest piece of work that you have undertaken to date. It is therefore important that you try to find an area that you enjoy learning about. There are things you can consider doing to help you identify an appropriate topic.

- It is likely that during your degree you will have enjoyed some topics or modules more than others or will have a particular interest in a certain group of children and/or young people or subject area. Think about what you really enjoy doing and learning about and try, if possible, to build your project around this. It will be much easier if you are researching something you are passionate about.

- You might also want to talk to colleagues within your school or setting to see if there is something that you can do which also addresses a need within your workplace. (This will be discussed more fully later within this chapter.)

- Another source of inspiration is to talk to other students on your course to see if any of their ideas spark your interest.

- Sometimes previous students' dissertations are available for you to look at. These might also resonate with something you are thinking of doing.

- You could also take on an additional challenge. Is there something that you have been quite sceptical about or an area of study where you have been unable to find research for one of your modules? This might be an area you consider studying.

What type of project do you want to undertake in your school/setting?

Once you have decided upon the area you want to research, you need to start 'reading around' the topic to get an understanding of what the literature says. The sooner you start doing this the better. Hopefully you will be researching something you already have an interest in so you may already be familiar with some of key literature and authors relating to the topic. You will need to complete a literature review when presenting your report so reading good quality literature is essential. Sources might include journal articles, books, reports, academic blogs and some websites. Remember this is an academic piece of writing, so you need to be careful about the websites and sources you use.

The type of setting and year group you are situated in might also influence what type of project you undertake, as could the time of year at which your project needs to be submitted. For example, it might be difficult to consider a topic such as 'parents' attitudes about the transition from primary to secondary school' if you are planning to carry out your research with the parents of children in Year 9. They might have forgotten many of the anxieties or the excitement their children felt three or four years ago.

Negotiating your project

If you are conducting your research in your school or setting you will most likely need to discuss your ideas with your headteacher or a member of the senior leadership team to get their agreement for the project to go ahead. In research terms this person is known as the 'gatekeeper' (Oliver, 2010) and their approval is needed as you will probably be undertaking research with your colleagues, parents or the children you work with. Negotiating a research project is not a linear process and even though you might have strong views about the project you want to carry out, the gatekeeper might want you to adapt your project. If you are already knowledgeable about the project you hope to carry out, you will be more confident in your negotiations and in turn the gatekeeper will have more confidence in you.

As already stated, it can be helpful in getting the agreement for your project to go ahead if the project can in some way be seen to benefit the school or setting. Many students we have worked with have undertaken an evaluation of an intervention the school has put in place. This serves the dual purpose of enabling you to undertake your research project, but also provides a useful resource for the school or setting. Having advocated negotiating a project which can benefit the setting, sometimes headteachers or colleagues have suggested students undertake projects which are much too large and complex to be appropriate for a small-scale research project. You will need to take advice from your tutors as to what is 'doable' as part of a small-scale research project.

CASE STUDY 13.1

Anne

I think one of the hardest parts of my research project was deciding what to do. There were so many things that I was interested in I couldn't make my mind up. I spoke to my tutors at university, colleagues at school but still couldn't decide. Then one day there was a visiting speaker at the university and they were talking about the 'phonic screening test'. At that point I was working with children in Year 1 doing a phonics intervention group. I knew that children achieving well in the phonic screening test was very important to the school and the children were beginning to pick up on this message. I wanted to find out how the children felt about the phonic screening test but it was important that I got the views of both the children who had passed and those who had 'failed'.

I discussed my ideas with the headteacher and the literacy co-ordinator and they were both happy for the research to go ahead so long as I did it sensitively with the children who had not passed the test first time. The findings from my research indicated that, although colleagues in school had tried very hard not to put pressure on the children to do well, the children were getting subliminal messages that the test was very important and were anxious about it. Until I talked to the children we didn't know just how 'big a deal' it was for the children and how it made them feel when they 'failed'.

When I had completed my research I fed back the findings to the headteacher and was asked to present it to the rest of the staff in a staff meeting and to the governors. It has resulted in a different approach to the phonic screening test within the school and although it is important we are much more mindful of how we work with the children.

It feels really good that my research has made a difference to practice, no matter how small that was, and I also got a good mark for my research project!

REFLECTION POINTS

■ What topics are you particularly interested in? Could this be a good area to research?

■ Is there an intervention taking place within your school/setting that would benefit from being evaluated?

■ Whose support could you enlist to help you decide upon an area to research?

What type of research approach will you take – case study or action research?

Case study research

One of the most common approaches taken to undertaking a small-scale research project is to carry out a case study (Yin, 2013). Case studies can gather quantitative or qualitative data or adopt a mixed-methods approach, although usually they will tend to lean towards qualitative or mixed-methods approaches. The case study method allows you to consider a problem or issue in depth (Simons, 2009). The researcher usually involves only a small number of participants and the study is very focussed. They will also usually adopt more than one method of data collection (interviews, observations, questionnaires, document analysis), allowing them to triangulate the data. One of the drawbacks of using this approach is that the data are very specific to the setting you are studying, meaning the findings are unique to that setting and are not therefore generalisable. However, there may be transferability to other similar groups and settings. There are some very good books on doing case studies in the recommended reading at the end of this section.

Action research

Action research has similar elements to a case study in that it allows the researcher to consider a problem or issue in depth. Again there may be more than one method of data collection. However, action research usually seeks to change or develop something to make improvements and one of the characteristics is that you will need to get other people within the setting 'on board'. It will usually adopt a cyclical or spiral approach. See figure 13.1.

It is seen as 'practitioner research' as it is often undertaken by people who have a vested interest in improving an area of practice (Baumfield et al., 2013).

Action research follows a similar pattern to a case study in that practitioners focus on an area of practice and **plan** how they feel they might improve it. They then **act** on this plan and some sort of change or intervention is put in place. The effects of this change are then **observed** and evaluated. The researchers will then **reflect** on the process and **plan** how they feel additional changes might be implemented to further improve practice. The cycle continues until researchers/practitioners feel no further improvements can be made.

However, there is a note of caution about carrying out action research as part of a project which needs to be completed fairly quickly. It can take several cycles to complete action research and therefore it can take several months or longer, and you may not have enough time to complete the project before your work needs to be submitted.

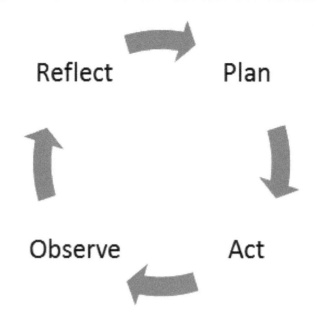

Figure 13.1 Action research cycle

REFLECTION POINT

■ Can you think of anything within your setting that has adopted this approach to evaluating its effectiveness?

Provision of a supervisor

It is possible that your university/college will provide a supervisor to help support you in undertaking your research project. Their advice and guidance in what is acceptable and appropriate in your institution will be invaluable as every institution has slightly different rules and regulations. You should remember that your supervisor is there to support you but it is your responsibility to contact them in order to gain the most from their knowledge and experience. Your supervisor should be able to help you think of and design a project which is realistic and able to be completed within the relevant timeframe. Your supervisor may also work with you to complete your research proposal and ethics approval forms (this will be discussed later in this chapter). They may also be marking your work so it will be beneficial to develop a good working relationship with them.

Designing a project that is 'doable'

Having supervised student research projects for over 14 years I have found that there are several common mistakes that students make. The first of these is that students often aim to undertake projects that are too broad initially. Often students will come to an initial meeting with a research question such as 'What is the best way to teach children to read?' If we had teams of researchers all over the world and millions of pounds to carry out the research we would not be able to address this question. Therefore, your research question needs to be focussed. You might adapt the question above to something along the lines of 'What strategies are used in a mainstream foundation stage unit to teach children to read?' Here you would be able to gather some data from colleagues within your setting and you could begin to address this question. If your focus is too broad then you will almost certainly be tempted to go off at a tangent and your research project will seem unwieldy. This is likely to cause you a great deal of stress and many sleepless nights worrying.

ACTIVITY

Let's use the question above: 'What strategies are used in a mainstream Foundation Stage unit to teach children to read?' You will need to develop two or three subsidiary questions to help you address the main research question. These might be:

■ What direct strategies do teaching staff employ to support children learning to read?

■ What activities are available to children within the setting that support the development of their reading skills?

■ What other strategies do the setting use to develop the children's reading skills?

Once you have decided upon your research question and your subsidiary questions, you will need ask yourself: What is the best way to find out the information to answer these questions?

For example: How might you go about finding the answer to the first subsidiary question above?

Answer:

You might have considered asking the teaching staff directly (interviews) or you might have decided to carry out some observations to see for yourself what

(continued)

(continued)

strategies the teaching staff use. You could use both of these methods of data collection or others.

Consider the remaining two subsidiary questions.

- ■ How might you find out the answers to these?

- ■ Who would you ask and why?

Secondly, students are often overambitious. They might aim to interview every member of staff and send a questionnaire to every parent within the school or involve several schools in their projects. This will not only be very time-consuming to carry out the research but will produce a mass of data that will be difficult to analyse. Try to focus on just one problem/year group/child/issue – this will go some way to ensuring that your project is 'doable' within the allotted timeframe.

Another common mistake that students can make is to 'go off at a tangent'. We are all intelligent people who enjoy researching and finding things out. It is really easy to get side-tracked and spend a lot of time investigating or reading things that are not related to our project. Some subsidiary research questions should help keep your research focussed but when you are working you might consider asking yourself 'How is what I am doing contributing to my research project?' If it isn't, then question whether you really do have time to pursue that line of enquiry. Of course, everything you learn will be valuable, but in terms of completing your project then try to be strict with yourself.

Some students have strong ideas about how they want to carry out their research before they have decided exactly what it is they want to do. I have worked with students who are determined that they want to send out questionnaires to parents before they have decided what exactly it is they want to research. It is important not to have preconceived ideas about how you want to collect your data or what you want to ask before you have decided upon your research questions. Your research questions and then your subsidiary questions need to come first. Only then can you decide the best way to collect your data and who should be your participants.

Getting other colleagues in school on board

Your project will be very important to you and will probably be a primary focus while you are undertaking it (at least in terms of your study). However, your colleagues might not be so enthusiastic about taking part and you need to remember that any research can be an intrusion into people's privacy, even if the topic is work related. Additionally, schools and educational settings are busy places and colleagues might say they are willing to be a participant in your study but when the time comes to take part they may find that they do not have the time. There are things you can do to help in this situation. Some ideas are listed below:

- Give people plenty of notice of interviews or focus groups.

- Be flexible.

- If you are conducting interviews or focus groups, consider whether to provide your participants with details of the questions in advance. This may also help alleviate any concerns they might have about what they are going to be asked.

- Send out reminders about questionnaires. Consider whether an electronic questionnaire might be more easily completed than a paper one.

The research proposal

Most universities/colleges require students to complete a research proposal. This is a detailed description about what you want to do and how you are going to carry out your research project. In some universities/colleges this aspect of your work is part of your assessment. However, even if preparing a formal research proposal is not a requirement of your institution, it is a very useful exercise to carry out independently as it will make you think through exactly what you are going to do. It will also provide a good basis for when you begin to write up your study. All institutions differ in what they require in a research proposal but some general headings that might be helpful include: proposed title; research aims; research questions; background to the project; sample; methods of data collection; limitations; and any perceived ethical issues.

Ethical review/approval

Most research projects undertaken as part of a degree programme will require ethical review/approval and virtually all research projects that involve human participants will require approval. Each institution will have its own procedures for ethical review and therefore it is extremely important that you find out and adhere to those laid down by your institution. Gaining ethics approval for your project may seem like another hurdle to be overcome, but it requires the researcher to consider the implications of the research for the participants, the institution and themselves. It also ensures that all parties represented are protected and particular care should be taken when carrying out research with children, young people and vulnerable adults.

Usually, you must have ethics approval before you conduct any research, although there are things which you may be able to prepare in advance such as questionnaires, information sheets for your participants, interview questions or schedules and written informed request forms. Some institutions require you to submit some or all of such documentation when you submit your application for ethics approval. Your supervisor will be able to advise you on the requirements of your institution.

Writing a research plan

If you fail to plan then you plan to fail.

The above quote has been attributed to many people such as Benjamin Franklyn and Winston Churchill, and it could not be truer of a research project. Unlike some of your other assignments, when it may have been possible for you to leave it to the last minute and then 'pull an all-nighter' this is not possible with a research project, as it requires work to be undertaken in stages.

As stated earlier your research project is probably the longest piece of written work that you will have undertaken to date. It is also probably the most complex piece of work that you have undertaken over the longest period of time. Creating and adhering to a research plan will help you keep your work organised and on track. It can also assist with making the project feel less daunting if it is broken down into smaller 'chunks'. I usually advise students to leave two weeks before the date of their final submission for them to make final edits to their work. It can be useful to work out how many weeks you have in which to undertake your research and plan what you need to do on a week-by-week basis. You will also need to take your other commitments into account, for example if you are required to contribute or write school reports or support students with SATs or other pressure points within the school/setting calendar. In the past I have advised students to create a grid system which is very visual and enables them to tick off tasks when they have been completed. This does of course presuppose that you know what you need to do. Your research proposal should have helped you clarify this in your own mind and you can also draw upon the knowledge and experience of your supervisor to help you create a timeline for your project. Each plan will be different but an example of how a section of plan might look is given below.

It is important that you plan and manage your project effectively. It may seem as if you have a great deal of time when you start undertaking your project but research is very time-consuming and it will soon slip by. It also is possible that you will have other assignments to undertake alongside your research project and it is important that you do not neglect these.

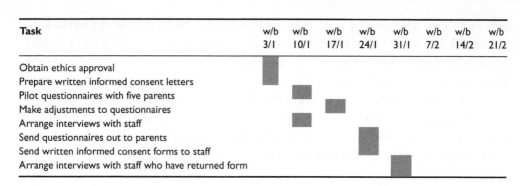

Task	w/b 3/1	w/b 10/1	w/b 17/1	w/b 24/1	w/b 31/1	w/b 7/2	w/b 14/2	w/b 21/2
Obtain ethics approval								
Prepare written informed consent letters								
Pilot questionnaires with five parents								
Make adjustments to questionnaires								
Arrange interviews with staff								
Send questionnaires out to parents								
Send written informed consent forms to staff								
Arrange interviews with staff who have returned form								

Figure 13.2 Example of an action plan

How it can help benefit your career

While undertaking a research project can be a little daunting at the time, many students have reported that it has enhanced their standing within the school where they are working. All of a sudden they are taking the lead on a project, seeking the opinions of colleagues/parents/students, compiling and sending out questionnaires and demonstrating they are very knowledgeable about current issues or initiatives.

Like Anne in the case study above, several past students have reported that they have been asked to present the findings from their research projects at staff meetings and to governors. Although nerve-racking at the time students almost always report that ultimately they enjoyed doing it and that it raised their profile within the school. This can be especially helpful if you want to continue with your studies and perhaps go into teaching at a later date. Schools have been known to employ existing staff en route to gaining qualified teacher status (QTS). This is discussed more fully in the next chapter.

Chapter summary

Within this chapter we have considered some strategies you might use to help you decide on an appropriate topic for you to study as part of your research project. We have also briefly looked at how any small-scale research project needs to be very focussed and you need to be very strict with yourself so that you do not get side-tracked. We have considered how important it is to get your headteacher or the leadership team on board with your project and how you might achieve this, as well as looking at some of the processes you may have to undertake in order to satisfied the requirements of your university such as completing a research proposal and ethics approval form. Planning is essential when undertaking a research project and we have looked at one idea as to how you might prepare a plan to keep your work on track. Undertaking a research project might also raise your profile in the school and you may be able to disseminate the findings from your research. While this may seem daunting, other students have reported that this has helped colleagues within their workplace to consider them in a different light.

Undertaking a research project will possibly be one of the most challenging pieces of work that you will undertake but students also report that it is often the most rewarding and they are rightly proud of their achievements.

FURTHER READING

Bell, J. and Waters, S. (2014) *Doing your research project: a guide for first time researchers*. Maidenhead: Open University Press.

Denscombe, M. (2014) *The good research guide: for small-scale social research projects*. Maidenhead: Open University Press.

Oliver, P. (2010) *The student's guide to research ethics*. Maidenhead: Open University Press.

References

Baumfield, V., Hall, E. and Wall, K. (2013) *Action research in education: learning through practitioner enquiry* (2nd edn). London: Sage.

Oliver, P. (2010) *The student's guide to research ethics*. Maidenhead: Open University Press.

Simons, H. (2009) *Case study research in practice*. London: Sage.

Yin, R. (2013) *Case study research: design and method*. London: Sage.

Next steps

Further developing your reflective practice; professional and academic learning; career progression

Lorraine Thomas

CHAPTER OVERVIEW AND AIMS

■ To outline the wider context of the reflective practice movement against the background of accountability in education and the socio-political landscape

■ To reflect on how your Foundation Degree studies have developed your professional and academic learning to support children and young people in schools

■ To explore next steps in further developing your professional and academic learning

■ To explore next steps in further developing your career progression, including routes into teaching

Introduction

This chapter will encourage you to recognise the value of detailed reflection on aspects of your practice, in order to make improvements that will ultimately have a positive impact on supporting children and young people in schools. The wider context of the reflective practice movement is discussed against the current background of accountability in education and the socio-political landscape. This chapter will also outline opportunities for further professional and academic learning, such as top-up awards to gain an honours degree. Gaining an honours degree opens up a range of career progression opportunities, including teaching, and this chapter will also discuss the different routes into teaching that are now available. Finally, this chapter will discuss the benefits of Master's level study, as many professionals working in education now undertake professional and academic learning at this higher level due to the complex demands of supporting children and young people in schools. Case studies will be used to exemplify further professional and academic learning as well as different pathways undertaken by others, outlining the impact they have had on their learning, practice and career progression.

Context

In order to reflect on your role in the wider context, it is important to understand the current background of accountability in education and the socio-political landscape, since 'there may be tensions between what you would *like* to do in the classroom and what you are *required* to do' (Thomas and Griggs 2011: 21). Such tensions in schools are typically between the drive for excellent academic outcomes / the 'value added' regarding academic outcomes, and innovative and creative curricula and approaches.

Until the latter part of the twentieth century, governments on the whole had left decision-making regarding education in the hands of professionals. In the 1980s, however, the old economic order changed: there was a sudden rise in oil prices; the collapse of the traditional manufacturing base; the development of new technologies, which made it possible to relocate manufacturing to countries where labour costs were cheaper; and an increasing deregulation of economies and financial markets (Thomas and Griggs, 2011). Consequently, governments and the public have become increasingly aware of the high cost of public services, such as education, and there has been a universal demand for 'value for money', leading to the introduction of a range of accountability and performance measures of professionals working in education. In education, these measures included the introduction of the Office for Standards in Education (Ofsted) – now known as the Office for Standards in Education, Children's Services and Skills (Ofsted) – under the Education (Schools) Act (1992), which led to:

- school inspections
- the publication of school league tables, and
- national standards for teachers (see DfE, 2012).

Concerns are often expressed that many schools in England are now dominated by testing, league tables and competition, but Wrigley (2006), for example, also reminds us that it does not have to be like this to provide meaningful learning for pupils.

REFLECTION POINTS

Think about the wider context of your work as discussed above and consider times when there have been tensions between what you would *like* to do and what you are *required* to do to support children and young people, in order to reflect on the following questions:

- How did you feel about the situation?

- What was the underlying issue for the tensions?

- How have your Foundation Degree studies supported you to recognise and address these tensions?

Professional and academic learning

Most professionals supporting children and young people in schools in the United Kingdom are entitled to 30 hours of mandatory continuing professional development (CPD), but this is low in comparison with some of the world's highest-performing school systems (McKinsey, 2007). Although the amount of CPD is low in England, there are also other concerns, including criticisms regarding the brevity of many typical, traditional methods of CPD, such as one-day training courses (Boyle *et al.*, 2005). More CPD is needed for those supporting children and young people in schools in the UK, but it is also essential to reconsider the nature of CPD. Kennedy (2005) considers that for CPD to be transformative it needs to include reflection, criticality and analysis, in addition to being in-depth and sustained. These features are typical of many higher education academic courses, which are designed to support children and young people in schools, and are underpinned by principles of reflective practice (Schön, 1983).

Lunenberg and Korthagen (2009: 235) affirm that 'Reflection seems the vital instrument for making the connections between experience, theory and practical wisdom.' Clearly, detailed reflection is the key that unlocks the interrelationship between experience, theory and practical wisdom. In the field of academic studies, it is not unusual for students working with children and young people in schools to regard their course as either overly theoretical or of limited practical value, unless this is effectively mediated in school, in order to address the gap between theory and practice. This suggests, therefore, that some students do not see the benefits of linking theory with practice and/or perhaps these links are not made explicit. It is the responsibility of educators, however, to interpret and apply theory in a manner conducive to building knowledge, which is both a solid foundation for future learning and can be applied in practice (Bruner, 1996). This is an important area, as the links between theory and practice are known to be problematic, yet practice can be greatly advanced if this issue is addressed effectively (Korthagen and Kessels, 1999). Also, integrating the role of the school in students' learning can improve the linkage between theory and practice (Simkins, 2009) and students also appear to recognise the efficacy of learning linked to the school context (Walker and Dimmock, 2006).

One contribution of higher education to your professional and academic learning may well have been to encourage you to support children and young people in schools within the social constructivist approach of the facilitation of learning (Vygotsky, 1962), in order to move beyond didactic instruction into facilitating interactive teaching styles, reflection and discussion. Another contribution may have been to encourage you to support young people in secondary schools within an andragogical approach (Knowles, 1990) – again promoting the facilitation of learning, but specifically relating to the motivation of adult learning.

REFLECTION POINTS

Brighouse and Woods (1999: 109) noted, in the context of school improvement, that 'tiny differences in input can quickly become overwhelming differences in output.' They call these small interventions 'butterflies', after the work on chaos theory that has produced the concept of 'the butterfly effect'. Consider the professional and academic learning as discussed above regarding your Foundation Degree, in order to reflect on the following questions:

- How have your foundation degree studies developed your professional and academic learning to further support children and young people in schools?

- How have you applied what you have learned in theory to support children and young people?

- How have you made improvements to your practice, which will ultimately have a positive impact on supporting children and young people?

- How have you grown personally, professionally and academically since starting to undertake your Foundation Degree?

Next steps

Successful completion of your Foundation Degree is a significant achievement. By now, hopefully you will have caught the lifelong learning bug and will want to learn more! So, what might your next steps be? There are lots of opportunities for further professional and academic learning, such as top-up awards to gain an honours degree. Gaining an honours degree opens up a range of career progression opportunities, including teaching. Information regarding top-up awards can be found on university websites and your Foundation Degree course co-ordinator will be able to discuss top-up awards with you in more detail. Your headteacher may also be able to fund or partially fund your top-up award, especially if you commit to undertaking a small-scale piece of research which will support school improvement or if you are considering progression to a teaching role.

Career progression

Support roles

Over recent years, there has been a vast increase in the number of people who support children and young people in schools and other educational settings, both as employees and as volunteers (Campbell and Fairburn, 2005). Around half of the school workforce comprises support staff, so there are currently lots of opportunities in primary schools, secondary schools and special schools. In particular, most support members of staff in support roles are teaching assistants, who can often progress as higher level teaching assistants. There are also other support roles in areas such as: administration, counselling, cover supervision, data and examinations, finance, human resources, library and resources, pastoral care, mentoring, and technical support.

CASE STUDY 14.1

Ruth

Ruth completed a BA (Hons) Early Childhood Studies in her late 30s. Driven by a love of books and literacy, she became a school library assistant, progressed to a secondary school librarian role and was then promoted to the post of Learning Resource Manager in a large multi-academy trust, which includes primary schools, secondary schools and a special school. As a manager, Ruth wanted to take her education to the next level and to develop her leadership and management skills, so undertook an MA in Education (Leadership and Management) as part of a school-based cohort alongside colleagues undertaking support and teaching roles. At work, this led to enhanced working relationships with colleagues in her cohort and the subsequent exchanging of

(continued)

(continued)

ideas. The MA in Education (Leadership and Management) gave her the opportunity to gain theoretical insight into her professional practice, afforded her personal growth regarding her ability to complete independent research and gain deeper critical thinking skills, developed her leadership and management skills, invigorated her enthusiasm for lifelong learning, and had a real impact on her future aspirations. Although she has not seen the same career progression as her teaching colleagues since completing her Master's degree, she recognises that it is impossible to compare opportunities for career progression in these two professions and so the lack of further progression was not unexpected. Ruth was very appreciative of her school funding the Master's course to enable her to develop her learning and skills. She is now planning to continue her learning at doctoral level via a PhD.

REFLECTION POINTS

- How do you feel those in support roles can best support children and young people?

- How do you feel those in support roles can best support children and young people with special educational needs and disabilities (SEND) in particular?

- What do you consider to be the advantages and disadvantages of support roles?

- What opportunities and challenges do you see for those in support roles?

Teaching

Teaching is a demanding, but very rewarding career. It is no wonder that so many inspirational and complimentary comments have been made about teaching. Dr John Cater (2017: 49), Vice Chancellor of Edge Hill University in England, asserts that 'There is no profession more important than teaching. Life chances are created and futures mapped, particularly for those from less advantaged backgrounds.' Teaching also has a clear salary and career progression structure. Furthermore, teachers are in high demand in the UK and beyond!

Gaining an honours degree opens up to you a career in teaching. You can enter teaching via several routes in England.

Most graduates in England and Wales enter teaching via a Level 6 Professional Graduate Certificate in Education (PGCE) or a level 7/ Master's level Postgraduate

Certificate in Education (PGCE), with recommendation for qualified teacher status (QTS). The PGCE is a very well-known academic award in education and has very high employability rates. The PGCE is also recognised in other parts of the UK and internationally, so if you think you may like to teach outside England in the future, it is important to undertake a PGCE. The PGCE is a one-year initial teacher education (ITE) higher education programme for graduates and has been a very successful and popular ITE programme since the 1950s. The Master's level PGCE was widely and successfully embedded within universities in England from 2007 and has high levels of student satisfaction (Thomas, 2013). Overall, the Master's level PGCE has brought ITE in England more in line with some of the highest-performing school systems such as Finland, where the notions of a Master's level teaching profession is considered to be a contributing factor to its success (Tryggvason, 2009). The Master's level PGCE is also considered by some to be the most appropriate route for the current demands on teachers (Sewell, 2008). It is essential to check entry criteria on university websites, but successful entry criteria to a PGCE in England and Wales are typically an honours degree at 2:2 or above; appropriate school experience of at least two weeks; passing the QTS skills tests in literacy and numeracy; and General Certificates in Secondary Education (GCSEs) at grade C or above in English, mathematics and science for the primary phase and English and mathematics for the secondary phase. You will also be interviewed to assess your suitability for the course and entry to the teaching profession. It is a rigorous process and essential that you prepare fully for the QTS skills tests and interview. Many universities will provide support in these areas and information can be gained via university websites or university careers advisors. Information regarding PGCE courses can be found on university websites, and the university's PGCE course co-ordinator will be able to discuss the course with you in more detail. PGCE awards are validated by universities and are often undertaken as a university-led course with at least two placements in schools, enabling you to develop your understanding of pedagogy and to put this into practice in the classroom. In England, PGCE awards can also be undertaken within a school-led course for schools working with universities as part of a School Direct school-centred initial teacher training (SCITT) or Teach First partnership.

Some graduates enter teaching via QTS-only routes. If you are an experienced unqualified teacher with an honours degree, the Assessment-Only route allows you to demonstrate that you already meet all of the standards for QTS. It is important to note, however, that QTS is not recognised in all other parts of the UK and internationally, so if you think you may like to teach outside England in the future, a QTS-only route is not advisable. If you do decide to undertake a QTS-only route, it is advisable for you to later complete an academic award in education. Some universities offer a PGCE without QTS, which is beneficial if you would like to teach outside England, and most universities offer higher qualifications in education, such as an MA in Education. Information regarding PGCE courses without QTS and MA Education courses can be found on university websites.

Some graduates enter teaching via an undergraduate route – either via a Foundation Degree and undergraduate ITE top-up award or via an undergraduate ITE course. Undergraduate ITE top-up awards and undergraduate ITE courses, with recommendation for QTS, are popular with many considering a career in teaching in primary schools in particular. Information can be found on university websites, and the university's undergraduate ITE course co-ordinator will be able to discuss this award with you in more detail.

CASE STUDY 14.2

Virinder

Virinder completed a Foundation Degree in Early Years to broaden and deepen her understanding of Early Years education and to gain practical experience. During the Foundation Degree, Virinder undertook a range of modules in areas such as child development, curriculum and creativity. Her placements in a nursery and a special school gave her the opportunity to put theory into practice and shaped her desire to become a teacher, so much so that she is now completing an undergraduate Primary ITE top-up award, with recommendation for QTS. The top-up award included teaching practice at Key Stage 2 (children aged from 7 to 11), which extended her knowledge and experience beyond Early Years and supported her to meet the Teachers' Standards (DfE, 2012); and enabled her to research teaching English creatively for her dissertation. Virinder is now planning to become a primary school teacher within a mainstream primary school or special school. She also has aspirations to undertake a leadership role in the future and to continue her learning via an MA in Education.

Finally, Master's level study has many benefits for supporting children and young people (see Denby *et al.*, 2008): supporting you in your lifelong learning and enhancing overall school improvement, if you choose an appropriate Master's degree designed with these aims (Wiliam, 2010). Also, for those of you aspiring to become a Special Educational Needs Co-ordinator (SENCO) in the future, the Postgraduate Certificate in Special Educational Needs for SENCOs and the National Award for SEN Co-ordination (NASC) are mandatory awards for newly-appointed SENCOs in their first three years. Information regarding the Postgraduate Certificate in Special Educational Needs for SENCOs and the National Award for

SEN Co-ordination can be found on university websites. Master's level study is beneficial in providing a professional language and confidence with which to articulate your practice (Thomas, 2017) and may also enhance your employability and career progression (Thomas, 2013).

Chapter summary

This chapter outlines the significant changes in the accountability in education and the socio-political landscape. Funding for schools is currently a very controversial issue, which also has a real impact on jobs, job security, CPD and career progression. Although career progression is more limited for those in support roles, there are several ways in which you can progress in your career and also advance your professional and academic learning, as outlined in this chapter. As a well-established profession, teaching has a clear salary and career progression structure, in addition to lots of opportunities in which you can continue to advance your professional and academic learning.

Whichever career pathway you take, we trust that your Foundation Degree studies have been rewarding and beneficial to you personally and professionally and we hope that you will continue as a lifelong reflective practitioner and learner. There are few roles as important as supporting the next generation of children and young people in schools and we wish you all the very best with your future learning and career!

FURTHER READING

Denby, N., Swift, H., Butroyd, R., Glazzard, J. and Price, J. (2008) *Masters level study in education.* Maidenhead: Open University Press.

McGregor, D. and Cartwright, L. (2011) (eds) *Developing reflective practice: a guide for beginning teachers.* Maidenhead: Open University Press.

Sewell, K. (ed.) (2008) *Doing your PGCE at M-level.* London: Sage.

References

Boyle, B., Lamprianou, I. and Boyle, T. (2005) 'A longitudinal study of teacher change: what makes professional development effective?' Report of the second year of the study. *School Effectiveness and School Improvement.* Vol. 16, No. 1, pp 1–27.

Brighouse, T. and Woods, D. (1999) *How to improve your school.* London: Routledge.

Bruner, J. (1996) *The culture of education.* Cambridge, MA: Harvard University Press.

Campbell, A. and Fairbairn, G. (eds) (2005) *Working with support in the classroom.* London: Paul Chapman.

Cater, J. (2017) *Whither teacher education and training?* Oxford: Higher Education Policy Institute.

Denby, N., Swift, H., Butroyd, R., Glazzard, J. and Price, J. (2008) *Masters level study in education*. Maidenhead: Open University Press.

Department for Education (DfE) (2012) *Teachers' standards*. London: Her Majesty's Stationery Office.

Education (Schools) Act (1992), c. *38*. Available at: http://legislation.gov.uk/ukpga/1992/38/contents

Kennedy, A. (2005) 'Models of continuing professional development: a framework for analysis'. *Journal of In-service Education*. Vol. 31, No. 2, pp 235–250.

Knowles, M.S. (1990) *The adult learner: a neglected species* (4th edn). Houston: Gulf Publishing Company, Book Division.

Korthagen, F. and Kessels, J.P.A. (1999) 'Linking theory and practice: changing the pedagogy of teacher education'. *American Educational Research Association*. Vol. 28, No. 4, pp 4–17.

Lunenberg, M. and Korthagen, F. (2009) 'Experience, theory, and practical wisdom in teaching and teacher education'. *Teachers & Teaching*. Vol. 15, No. 2, pp 225–240.

McKinsey & Company (2007) *How the world's best-performing schools come out on top*. http://mckinsey.com/locations/ukireland/publications/pdf/Education_report.pdf (Accessed: 15 March 2018).

Schön, D.A. (1983) *The reflective practitioner: how professionals think in action*. New York: Basic Books.

Sewell, K. (ed.) (2008) *Doing your PGCE at M-level*. London: Sage.

Simkins, T. (2009) 'Integrating work-based learning into large-scale national leadership development programmes in the UK'. *Educational Review*. Vol. 61, No. 4, pp 391–405.

Thomas, L. (2013) 'An analysis of PGCE models: key stakeholder perceptions from the secondary phase'. *Teacher Education Advancement Network Journal*. Vol. 5, No. 3, pp 4–16.

Thomas, L. (2017) 'The masters in teaching and learning: lessons to be learnt and key stakeholder perceptions'. *Teacher Education Advancement Network Journal*. Vol, 9, No. 1, pp 45–55.

Thomas, L. and Griggs, G. (2011) 'How do you become a reflective professional?', in D. McGregor and L. Cartwright (eds), *Reflective practice: a guide for beginning teachers*. Maidenhead: Open University Press.

Tryggvason, M-T. (2009) 'Why is Finnish teacher education successful? Some goals Finnish teacher educators have for their teaching'. *European Journal of Teacher Education*. Vol. 32, No. 4, pp 369–382.

Vygotsky, L. (1962) *Thought and language*. Cambridge, MA: M.I.T. Press.

Walker, A. and Dimmock, C. (2006) 'Preparing leaders, preparing learners: the Hong Kong experience'. *School Leadership and Management*. Vol. 26, No. 2, pp 125–147.

Wiliam, D. (2010) *Teachers TV: masters in teaching and learning*. Available at: https://tes.com/teaching-resource/teachers-tv-masters-in-teaching-and-learning6044514 (Accessed: 15 March 2018).

Wrigley, T. (2006) *Another school is possible*. California: Bookmarks.

Index